Walther Ziegler

AF220317

Kafka
in 60 Minutes

Translated by
Alexander Reynolds

My thanks go to Rudolf Aichner for his tireless critical editing; Silke Ruthenberg for the fine graphics; Lydia Pointvogl, Eva Amberger, Christiane Hüttner, and Dr. Martin Engler for their excellent work as manuscript readers and sub-editors; Prof. Guntram Knapp, who first inspired me with enthusiasm for philosophy; and Angela Schumitz, who handled in the most professional manner, as chief editorial reader, the production of both the German and the English editions of this series of books.

My special thanks go to my translator

Dr Alexander Reynolds.

Himself a philosopher, he not only translated the original German text into English with great care and precision but also, in passages where this was required in order to ensure clear understanding, supplemented this text with certain formulations adapted specifically to the needs of English-language readers.

I live in my family, among the best and most lovable people, more strange than a stranger.[1]

Bibliographic Information held by the German National Library: The details of the original German edition of this publication are held by the German National Library as part of the German National Bibliography; detailed bibliographical data can be found online at www.dnb.de.

© 2022 Dr Walther Ziegler
1st Edition August 2022
Jacket design and graphic design for the whole book: Silke Ruthenberg, making use of illustrations by:
Raphael Bräsecke, Creactive – Studio for Advertising, Comics & Illustrations
© JackF - Fotolia.com (image-frames)
© Valerie Potapova - Fotolia.com (image-frames)
© Svetlana Gryankina - Fotolia.com (speech-balloons)

Production and publishing:
BoD - Books on Demand, Norderstedt
ISBN 978-3-7562-9519-7

Contents

Bibliographical References

Kafka's Great Discovery

Kafka (1883-1924) is not a philosopher but an author of literature. Nevertheless, he must be counted among the most important thinkers in world history. There is no incongruity in placing him in the company of Plato, Confucius, Kant, Hegel, Hume, Freud, Wittgenstein and Sartre. Because we owe to Kafka not just an outstandingly compelling part of the global literary heritage but also a philosophical discovery of timeless validity.

Kafka succeeded as very few others have in penetrating to the very core of what it is to exist as a human being. His writing reveals, in the most impressive possible way, just what it is that makes up Man's innermost essence, what it is that keeps us alive. His novels and short stories circle constantly around one key phenomenon: that of human empathy. A hardworking travelling salesman finds himself transformed one morning into an insect and becomes an object of contempt for his own family; a seasoned ship's pilot is suddenly driven away from the wheel by a total stranger amidst the dismaying inaction of his crew; a man wakes up one morning to find himself on trial for a crime that is never named to him; a son finds himself senselessly condemned to death by his own father. Always in Kafka the empathy of man with man, or rather more often the crying lack of it, is the theme.

One might put it another way and say that in all his novels and short stories Kafka directs an incorruptible gaze upon the extreme fragility of the relations that bind man to fellow man. No one can compare with him in the acuity of his grasp of how human beings depend upon one another, in every way, for their very existence:

> They are tied together by ropes and it's bad enough when the ropes around an individual loosen and he drops somewhat lower than the others into empty space; ghastly when the ropes break and he falls.[2]

Human beings, Kafka believes, are bound together as mountain climbers are bound together by ropes.

In this way we keep one another secure in our existences. Our hold on life, from start to finish, depends on that "granting of being" to us that takes the form of other people's recognition and acknowledgment of us as humans like them. But such a radical dependency on recognition and acknowledgment by others means, of course, that our whole existence is exposed to the terrible danger that this recognition and acknowledgment might not be, or might suddenly cease to be, accorded. Where this happens, be it in the form of an excommunication or of a social ostracism even to the point of an individual's becoming "dead to" those around him, a terrible abyss opens up before the individual thus let fall into "empty space".

This, then, is Kafka's great philosophical discovery: the fundamental necessity of mutual recognition and acknowledgment and the essential fragility, for all that, of this vital structure. But he reveals this discovery to us not from the distanced perspective of the philosopher or the scientist but from the "inside", intimate viewpoint of his literary creations and their individual experiences. Like the protagonists of his novels and short stories Kafka himself suffered terribly from feelings of social abandonment, of lack of recognition as a human being, and from the fundamental sense of "having no foothold in being" that goes hand in hand with these things:

> Last night, as I lay sleepless and let everything veer continually back and forth between my aching temples [...] what I had almost forgotten became clear to me: namely, on what frail ground, or rather

> altogether non-existent ground, I live, over a darkness out of which the dark power emerges when it wills and [...] destroys my life.[3]

> I could live and I do not live.[4]

Kafka is an author, a storyteller. But his stories provide much more than just entertainment. They initiate a process in the reader. Despite the variety of their topics they nearly all centre on one and the same thematic core. They draw us into the whirlpool of our own dreams, moods and anxieties. Whoever really engages with Kafka's writings will end up, in the end, coming face to face with himself and, whether he wants it or not, with the fragility of his own life. Kafka shows us how helplessly exposed we are to powers which we can barely, or not at all, control. He reveals to us the most radically unprotected dimensions of our existence and leads us into regions which, normally, we neither enter nor wish to enter.

There can be no question, then, but that Kafka brought to light in these writings also a profound philosophical truth. His stories and scattered thoughts push forward into a sphere of human existence which, for all the emphasis laid here on abandonment, indifference or even the threat posed to man by man, still nonetheless casts a clear light upon the possibility of a form of human community which would not be afflicted by any of these things. Kafka himself saw himself as someone treading, his whole life long, the border between these two worlds of isolation and community:

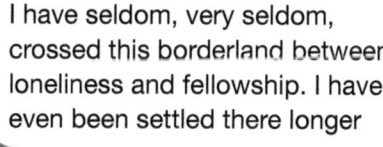

I have seldom, very seldom, crossed this borderland between loneliness and fellowship. I have even been settled there longer

than in loneliness itself. What a fine bustling place was Robinson Crusoe's island in comparison![5]

Perhaps the reason that Kafka was able so grippingly and precisely to portray this lack of true fellowship, and of all that makes interpersonal relations truly successful relations, was because this very lack had almost been his destruction. Already as a very young man, in 1903, he had written to a friend:

When you stand in front of me and look at me, what do you know of the griefs that are in me and what do I know of yours? And if I were to cast myself down before you and weep and tell you, what more would you

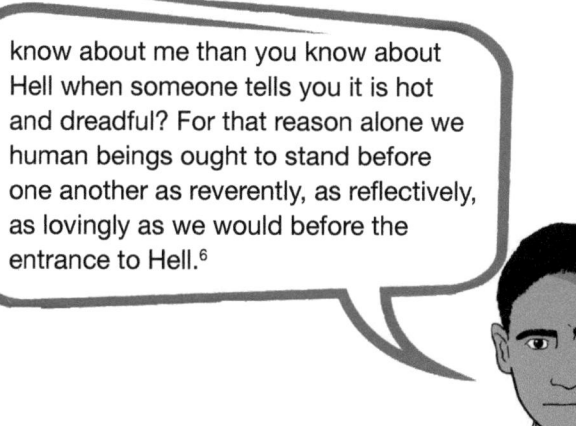

know about me than you know about Hell when someone tells you it is hot and dreadful? For that reason alone we human beings ought to stand before one another as reverently, as reflectively, as lovingly as we would before the entrance to Hell.[6]

Already at this early point in his life a schoolmate described Kafka as someone who seemed separated from all around him as if by a "glass wall".[7] An atmosphere of alienation and exposure to dark, threatening powers emerges and re-emerges so constantly and consistently in his works that posterity has coined the term "Kafkaesque" to evoke precisely such a mood of baffling but pervasive menace.

The Oxford English Dictionary states that "Kafkaesque" is "a word used to describe a situation that is confusing and frightening, especially one involving complicated official rules that do not seem to make any sense"[8]. Other dictionaries and lexica use such terms as "elusive" and "intangible" to describe the "dark power" that pervades both Kafka's private and his published writings. In the last analysis, however, the attempt to understand what is "Kafkaesque" without actually immersing oneself in Kafka's stories and other creations must be a vain one. "Kafkaesque", in the end, is just that aspect of our experience of the world that shows forth in the events and personalities described by Kafka.

But to what extent can we really say that this pervasive mood of Kafka's literary world contains a core philosophical idea? Can it really make sense to want to interpret Kafka philosophically? He does, after all, describe in his stories what are above all emotional "states of exception" of a kind which we know more from our nightmares than from anything experienced in everyday life. Is it really plausible, then, to take Kafka's subversively dream-like descriptions of interpersonal relations as a starting point for a philosophical analysis?

Much suggests that it is very plausible. Because, often, it is precisely a human experience that is wanting or lacking in some way that provides the best foundation for a description of interpersonal relations as they really should be. Attempts, indeed, have already been made by professional philosophers such as the Existentialist Sartre or the philosopher of religion

Martin Buber to analyse the basic structure of such interpersonal relations. But these philosophers were not able to render the key phenomena of the "inter-human" experienceable to their readers in anything like the vividness and immediate impressiveness that the literary genius Kafka renders it in. There is no doubt, then, that to understand Kafka is to understand the essential structure of human relations.

This said, however, it must also be said that the thoughts expressed by Kafka's protagonists tend to have something strangely dry, emotionless, almost business-like about them. Kafka differs from many authors who enjoy a similar level of fame in that his stories seldom evoke any sense of pathos. These stories awaken, nonetheless, strong feelings and this is perhaps because the figures in Kafka's writings tend to accept with a strange stoicism their often terrible fates. Kafka's descriptions of the inevitable failures and disasters of his various protagonists is seductive above all through its sober, almost distanced manner of observation and it is perhaps precisely through this that it provides the phenomenological basis for an extraordinary philosophical discovery.

Is it possible that the human individual is, under the surface of his proudly displayed self-confidence and self-awareness, no more than a feather in the winds of his relationships, present and past, with family, friends and society? In fictive scenario after scenario Kafka reveals to us the fragility of that system of relationships that sustains our normal life. And even if, in this normal life, we do not find ourselves suddenly transformed into a beetle or have abrupt sentence of death passed on us by our own parents, we nonetheless feel, as readers, all the uncanny force of such vilifications and excommunications. Kafka was fully aware of the cathartic effect of his works:

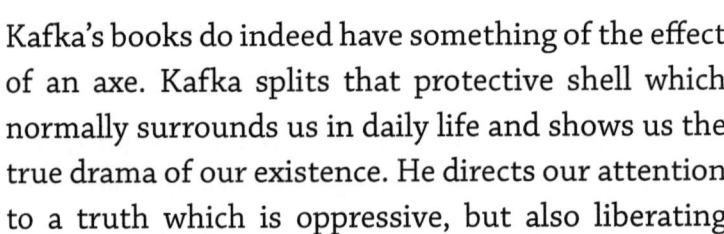

We need books that affect us like a disaster, that grieve us deeply, like the death of someone we loved more than ourselves, like being banished into forests far from everyone [...] A book must be the axe for the frozen sea inside us.[9]

Kafka's books do indeed have something of the effect of an axe. Kafka splits that protective shell which normally surrounds us in daily life and shows us the true drama of our existence. He directs our attention to a truth which is oppressive, but also liberating inasmuch as it reveals, along with the dangers, the opportunities for a humanity lived out together, illuminating above and beyond this the entire basic anthropological structure of the relation between man and man.

In the pages that follow we will attempt to describe and explain this essential truth discovered by Kafka, using examples drawn from his novels and from his longer and shorter stories. In what exactly does the fate of his protagonists consist? On what exactly do their lives founder and go under? Does this "foundering and going under" take one consistent form throughout the whole of Kafka's literary creation? How is it that we have a sense that the fantastic disasters which befall Kafka's characters are ones which we are intimately familiar with, from our own experiences and our dreams? And can one somehow perhaps deduce, from the forms of failure and disaster that Kafka describes, some idea of how a genuinely "successful" human co-existence would look? Could it be that Kafka, in the end, gives us the key to an understanding of the ontological structure of interpersonal relations?

In any case, he certainly takes us, in each of his stories, on a journey – a journey into our own inner selves.

Kafka's Central Idea

The Metamorphosis –
The Monstrousness of Love

Among Kafka's many short- and medium-length stories the one most read and best known is probably that bearing the significant title *The Metamorphosis*. Its shocking, disorienting opening sentence is a landmark in world literature:

> As Gregor Samsa woke one morning from uneasy dreams, he found himself transformed into some kind of monstrous vermin.[10]

At the opening of this famous story we find the commercial traveller Gregor Samsa lying helplessly on his strange new hard-shelled back and staring in astonishment at the thin insect legs now flickering before his eyes. Only after several vain attempts does he succeed in rolling himself out of bed and setting himself on his many feet. He proves unable, however, to raise himself up far enough to turn the key in his bedroom door and get out into the family apartment. He is also given no time to accustom himself to his new body before the chief clerk of the firm he is employed by officiously forces his way into the Samsa family home and begins to demand of him, through the still-locked bedroom door, an explanation for his failure to turn up at the office:

"Herr Samsa," the chief clerk now called with his voice raised, "What's going on? You're barricading yourself in your room, [...] causing your parents severe, unnecessary worries,

and neglecting – this just by the by – your business obligations in a quite unheard-of way [...] And your position is by no means the most secure."[11]

Gregor attempts to excuse his impropriety and to assure the chief clerk that he will sort things out but he finds that the people on the other side of the door hear, when he speaks, only the piping, distorted voice of an animal:

"Could you understand a single word?" the chief clerk was asking his parents. "He's not making a fool of us, is he?" "For heaven's sake!" his mother cried, "perhaps he's seriously ill!" […] "Grete! Grete!" she

screamed. "Yes, mother," called his sister from the other side […] "You must go to the doctor's this instant."[12]

When Gregor picks up through the door the news that a doctor and even a locksmith have been called, the latter to free him and the former to cure him, he at first feels great relief:

He felt drawn back into the sphere of humanity and had high hopes of impressive and surprising achievements from both the doctor and the locksmith.[13]

If he can only succeed in getting out of his bedroom, Gregor thinks, he will be taken up once again into the community of fellow creatures. But the opposite turns out to be the case. When he finally manages to wrestle the door open with his insect jaws, he is not "drawn back into the sphere of humanity", as he had hoped, at all. Instead, his mother reacts with blind terror, the chief clerk flees in panic from the house, and his own father takes up a stick and beats him back into his bedroom:

None of Gregor's pleas helped; none of his pleas was understood. However submissively he turned his head, his father stamped all the more vigorously with his feet [...] hissing like a savage. As yet, Gregor had had no practice at all in moving backwards and it was really very

slow going [...] He was afraid of making his father impatient if he tried the time-consuming manoeuvre (of turning around) and every moment the stick in his father's hand threatened him with a fatal blow on his back or on his head.[14]

Finally, Gregor succeeds in turning around and making his way back toward the bedroom. But his new body proves too broad for the narrow door. He needs, in order to re-enter the room, to follow the same procedure as he had in leaving it: crawl up the doorframe until he is on his lowest legs and then squeeze himself through the doorway inch by inch. But he already feels that his father will not have the patience to put up with such a long, slow manoeuvre:

(His father) would never have permitted the elaborate preparations that Gregor needed to pull himself upright and perhaps get through the door that way [...] Behind Gregor, it no longer sounded like the voice of one single father merely; it was really no longer a joke by now

and Gregor forced himself – come what may – into the doorway [...] Soon, he was stuck fast [...] His legs, on one side, stood quivering up in the air; those on the other side were pressed painfully down on the floor. Then his father gave him a vigorous kick from behind, which was truly a deliverance and he flew, bleeding heavily, into the depths of his room.[15]

With Gregor's "metamorphosis", then, not only is his own life transformed overnight but also the life of his whole family. This above all because, prior to this metamorphosis, Gregor had supported his family through his hard and conscientious work as a commercial traveller, allowing them to rent a large apartment and employ a cook and a cleaning woman. Gregor's transformation means that the family must now once again shift for themselves.

Gregor's sister Grete initially hopes that her brother will soon be "cured" and turn back once again into his former self. She brings him the only sorts of foods he finds himself able to eat, such as milk and half-rotten leftovers from the family meals. But even Grete avoids actually looking at him as she lays these dishes down.

Gregor too, initially, is full of understanding for the difficulty the family must have in accustoming themselves to his new and surely frightening outer form. He also accepts that the family have locked him in his bedroom, since, so he tells himself, they cannot know that he is still of the best intentions toward them. His sister, then, takes to giving warnings of her entry with his meals by rattling the key loudly in the lock, so that Gregor can hide under the sofa and spare her the sight of him. Once, when she arrives earlier than usual and he is not able to hide himself in time, she shrinks back in horror:

He understood from this that the sight of him was still intolerable to her and was bound to remain intolerable for the future [...].[16]

His mother, who has hitherto followed the advice of the family and "sensibly" refrained from visiting her son, falls into a faint when she encounters Gregor suddenly in the course of moving the furniture out of his room. Gregor in fact deliberately emerges from his hiding place in order to draw attention to himself and prevent that his room be emptied out completely. He concedes, in his mind, the fact that the family still means well by him and that, in his present state, he no longer needs furniture. But he develops a strong urge to retain at least a picture that had hung in the room. He fears that a completely empty room would be a "lair" in which "his human past would be consigned to utter oblivion". His sister, however, shows no understanding for these reservations. Seeing him settling himself dumbly down on the picture he wishes to keep in the room, prompting the terri-

fied mother's fainting fit, causes her to burst out at
him:

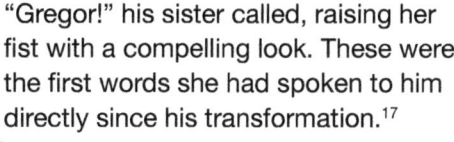

"Gregor!" his sister called, raising her
fist with a compelling look. These were
the first words she had spoken to him
directly since his transformation.[17]

Gregor's father, just returning from work at this
point, is also angered by the incident. When Grete
speaks of her brother having "broken out" he feels
compelled to drive him furiously back into the empty bedroom. In doing so, he begins to throw apples
from the living-room fruit bowl at him. The first
skims harmlessly off

[...] but the one that flew straight after it
literally penetrated Gregor's back. Gregor
tried to drag himself on further, as if the
surprising, unbelievable pain would pass
with a change of place. But he felt as if he

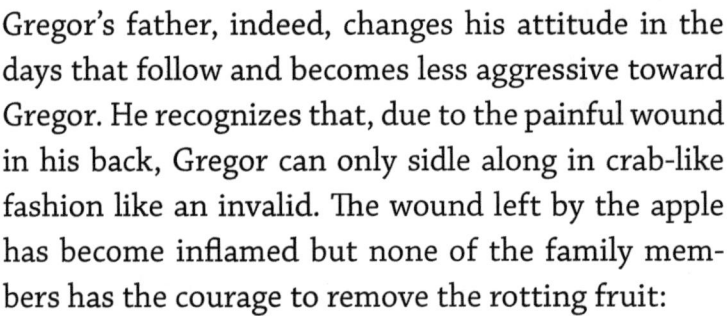

were nailed fast [...] Only with his last glance he was still able to see how the door to his room was flung open and his mother rushed forward [...] to their father [...] and begged him to spare Gregor's life.[18]

Gregor's father, indeed, changes his attitude in the days that follow and becomes less aggressive toward Gregor. He recognizes that, due to the painful wound in his back, Gregor can only sidle along in crab-like fashion like an invalid. The wound left by the apple has become inflamed but none of the family members has the courage to remove the rotting fruit:

Gregor's wound was serious and gave him pain for over a month [...]

but it seemed to have reminded even his father that, despite his present sad and repulsive form, Gregor was a member of the family who was not to be treated as an enemy; instead, family duty toward him commanded that they should swallow their disgust and put up with him in patience, just put up with him. And even though it

seemed that his wound had made Gregor lose his mobility for ever [...] he drew some recompense for this deterioration in his condition, one he considered was entirely adequate: toward evening, the

door to the living-room [...] was always opened so that, lying in the darkness of his room, invisible from the living-room, he might see the whole family at the lamp-lit table and hear what they had to say [...].[19]

This concession allowing him to take part again, even if only passively, in the life of the family is one that Gregor greatly appreciates. It gives him hope but proves in the end to lead only to still greater disaster. One evening, he is listening in this way to his sister playing violin in the living-room. She had, since her brother's "metamorphosis", given up playing the violin entirely and Gregor is deeply moved to hear her play again. He feels himself, indeed, so strongly drawn to the music that he begins to edge forward out of the shadow of his room:

> He resolved to advance right up to his sister, pluck her by the skirt to intimate that he was asking her to come with her violin into his room, for no one here was rewarding her playing as he would reward it [...] and he would confide to her his firm intention of sending her to the conservatoire [...] if this misfortune hadn't gotten

> in the way [...] After this explanation his sister would burst into tears of emotion and Gregor would rear up as far as her shoulders and kiss her throat [...].[20]

These expectations and the charm of his sister's playing revive Gregor's vital spirits and will to live. Full of hope, he edges forward toward his beloved sister but is discovered by her before he has gotten very far:

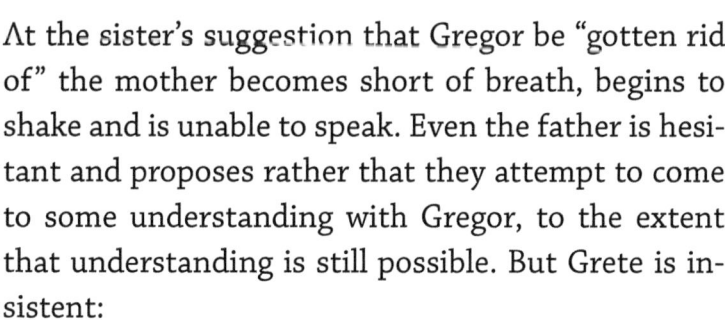

The violin fell silent [...] "Parents dear," said his sister, "it can't go on like this. I will not utter my brother's name in front of this monster and so will simply say: we must try to get rid of it. We have tried everything humanly possible [...] I don't think anyone can reproach us in the slightest for that."[21]

At the sister's suggestion that Gregor be "gotten rid of" the mother becomes short of breath, begins to shake and is unable to speak. Even the father is hesitant and proposes rather that they attempt to come to some understanding with Gregor, to the extent that understanding is still possible. But Grete is insistent:

> "It has to go [...] That is the only way, father. You must just try to get rid of the thought that it is Gregor [...] If it were Gregor he would have understood long ago that it's just not possible for human beings to live with a beast like that and he would have left of his own free will."[22]

Gregor, shocked by his sister's reaction, drags himself back into his room. He has no sooner succeeded, with great effort, in doing this, than he hears the sister, who had initially shrunk back from his laborious movements on the living-room floor, spring up behind him, slam and lock the door and cry out "Finally!" Gregor lies there wondering at the fact that, whereas the way into the living-room had seemed to him, drawn as he was by the music, so extremely easy, the way back out of it seems to have cost him all the strength he has left:

He soon discovered he was no longer able to move at all.[23]

He collapses, then, from exhaustion. To his relief, however, he also feels how, from this point on, those pains begin to vanish which have, over the preceding weeks, been making every movement a torture to him:

He could scarcely feel the apple in his back, rotten by now, nor the inflammation around it, covered all over in a thin film of dust. He thought back on his family with affection and love. His own opinion that he should vanish was, if anything, even more determined than his sister's.

He remained in this state of vacant and peaceful reflection (until) his head sank down without his willing it and from his nostrils his last breath faintly flowed.[24]

When, the following morning, the family's cleaning lady finds him there she at first believes that he is only pretending to be asleep or is "sulking". Soon, however, she becomes curious and begins to tickle him with her broom. When he does not react, she becomes annoyed and begins to push Gregor's body violently about the empty room with the broom. Finally, she realizes that Gregor is dead and passes on, in a loud and triumphant tone, the "good news" to the family:

"Come and see. It's snuffed it. It's lying in there, snuffed it. Completely."[25]

The closing sentence of Kafka's *Metamorphosis* is as legendary as its opening one. In their enormous relief at this new situation, Gregor's parents and sister decide all to take a day off from their respective employments. They send excuses to their employers and climb into a tram that runs out of the city into the countryside. The spring sun is shining brightly through the tram windows and they recognize with satisfaction that their ways of earning their livelihood are perhaps not so arduous after all. The family in fact now begins already to make plans to move into an apartment that will be smaller but, along with that, also better situated and more reasonably priced. As they ride along, the gaze of the parents comes to rest upon their daughter, illuminated by the beams of the spring sun. In the course of the family's ordeal, they suddenly notice, Grete has reached the age of womanhood. She is now old enough to marry and looks to make a fine wife for some young man:

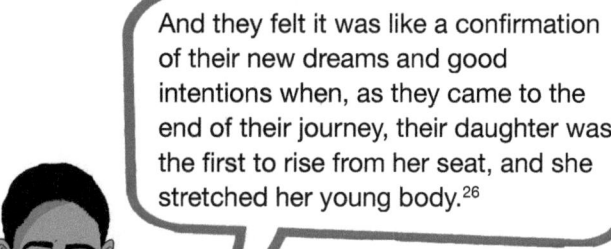

And they felt it was like a confirmation of their new dreams and good intentions when, as they came to the end of their journey, their daughter was the first to rise from her seat, and she stretched her young body.[26]

With this image of the "stretching of the young body" Kafka establishes a final contrast to the dried-out, dust-covered corpse of Gregor.

This novella-length short story of Kafka's, *The Metamorphosis*, really requires, in the end, no interpretation. It explains itself. The outward action, indeed, describes the transformation of Gregor Samsa, employed as a commercial traveller, into a gigantic beetle. The inner action – and what matters for Kafka is this inner action above all – shows us the psychological consequences of this transformation. In forfeiting his function as representative and breadwinner of the family Gregor Samsa also forfeits all the human affection and attachment associated with this function. For a time he is grudgingly tolerated; then the mood of the family turns decidedly against him. He is locked up, excommunicated and, in the end, declared "dead to the world" even before he dies:

"It has to go [...]"[27]

The Metamorphosis is nowadays one of the most famous works of literature of the modern period, known all over the world. It has such a gripping effect on the reader because its protagonist Gregor Samsa remains, right up till the end, attached to his family "with affection and love", even though the other members of this family cease to return this love and affection in any form at all. In essence, we may say, what Kafka shows us here is "the monstrousness of love".

The Helmsman – We Are All Replaceable

Also in another story of Kafka's we see a relationship which has endured for years dissolve, from one moment to the next, into thin air. The story is in this case a much shorter one: *The Helmsman*, which covers barely a page as against *The Metamorphosis*'s few dozen pages. The protagonist of *The Helmsman*, however, much like Gregor Samsa, finds himself robbed of his function and robbed as well, in and through this loss of his function, also of the very right to existence. The story, as we have said, fits in its entirety on one small page:

"Am I not the helmsman here?" I called out. "You?" asked a tall, dark man and passed his hands over his eyes as though to banish a dream. I had been standing at the helm in the dark night, a feeble lantern burning

over my head, and now this man had come and tried to push me aside. And as I would not yield, he put his foot on my chest and slowly crushed me while I still clung to the hub of the helm, wrenching it around

in falling. But the man seized it, pulled it back in place, and pushed me away. I soon collected myself, however, ran to the

hatchway that gave onto the mess quarters, and cried out: "Men! Comrades! Come here quick! A stranger has driven me away from the helm!" Slowly they came up, climbing the companion ladder, tired, swaying, powerful figures. "Am I the helmsman?" I asked. They nodded, but

they had eyes only for the stranger, stood around him in a semi-circle, and when, in a commanding voice, he said "Don't disturb me!", they gathered together,

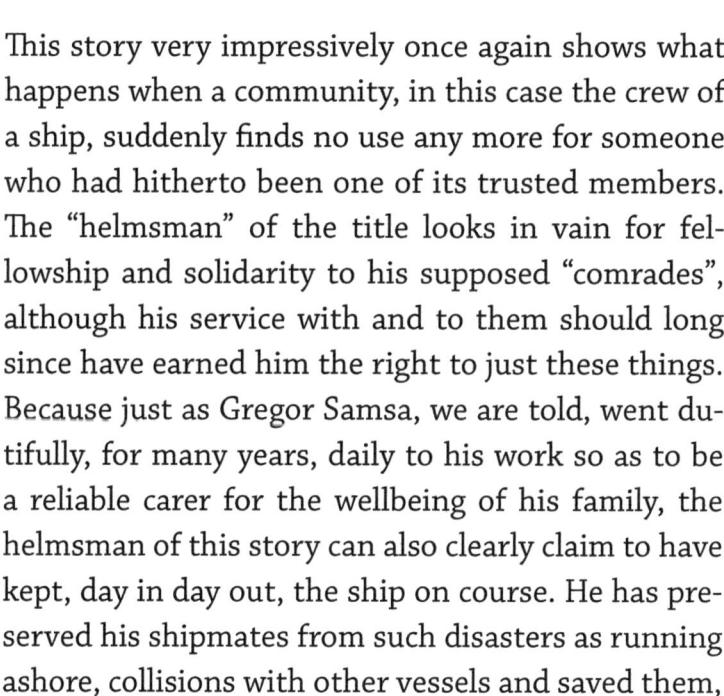

nodded at me, and withdrew down the companion ladder. What kind of people are these? Do they

ever think, or do they only shuffle pointlessly over the earth?[28]

This story very impressively once again shows what happens when a community, in this case the crew of a ship, suddenly finds no use any more for someone who had hitherto been one of its trusted members. The "helmsman" of the title looks in vain for fellowship and solidarity to his supposed "comrades", although his service with and to them should long since have earned him the right to just these things. Because just as Gregor Samsa, we are told, went dutifully, for many years, daily to his work so as to be a reliable carer for the wellbeing of his family, the helmsman of this story can also clearly claim to have kept, day in day out, the ship on course. He has preserved his shipmates from such disasters as running ashore, collisions with other vessels and saved them, above all, from drowning. They have been able to rely on him one hundred per cent. He has always been there for them: their helmsman in the truest sense. But then comes the moment when he needs their support, and asks them

"Am I the helmsman?"[29]

His shipmates nod, indeed, at first, in apparent agreement that he is. But then, instead of helping to remove the man who has forced himself illegitimately into this position, they remain passive and seemingly indifferent. When the stranger commands them "Don't disturb me" they accept this command without protest and climb back down into the mess quarters from which they had emerged.

Kafka's story is usually interpreted in one of three ways. Firstly, in economic terms: we are all, in modern society, dispensable and exchangeable. And as soon as we do indeed find ourselves, in whatever firm, corporation, or association we may be part of, displaced and replaced by someone else, any fellowship or relation of mutual trust and confidence as may have seemed to exist previously between ourselves and our colleagues or associates proves quickly to have been mere illusion. This holds true no less at managerial level than for the most menial of employees. The famous saying "The king is dead! Long live the king!" is perhaps even more applicable in today's working world than it was in the age of absolutism.

A second possible way of reading the story sees its message as above all a political one. This is perhaps most clearly and strongly legible out of the story's concluding line:

> What kind of people are these? Do they ever think, or do they only shuffle pointlessly over the earth?[30]

The crewmen display a reprehensible thoughtlessness in the way they go through life, inasmuch as they seem to be completely unconcerned about just what goals and intentions this new, intruding helmsman might have, or about whether he even has the ability to perform the job he has arrogated to himself. He appears to have convinced them just by his authoritarian attitude alone, presenting his claim to power and control as if it were something that simply went without saying. *The Helmsman*, consequently, is often interpreted as a warning to political democracies not to overestimate the cognitive capacities of their citizens. These citizens are often all too easily impressed and imposed upon by authoritarian personalities whenever these latter make their appearance.

Finally, there is also an autobiographical interpretation which would see Kafka attempting, in this story, to work through his own very difficult relationship with his father. On this interpretation, the helmsman would represent Kafka himself, whose intended way through life was being blocked and rendered impossible by his dominant and irascible father.

But if one sets aside these three attempts at interpretation and focuses in on the content and substance of the tale alone it is clear that this story too consists, in essence, in a simple and self-evident indication of the true structure of inter-human relations. Mutual trust and standing by one another form, on the high seas, the essential foundation of all fellowship and community. But the helmsman's having stood, for years, by his crew proves, in the end, to be worth nothing. His comrades, with whom he had felt there existed a meaningful bond, drop him as suddenly and brutally as Gregor Samsa had been dropped by his family. True closeness between the helmsman and his shipmates has ceased to exist and perhaps it had never existed. This is the true scandal related in Kafka's story.

A Hunger Artist –
Honoured, Misrecognized, Forgotten

The lack of human closeness is also the essential theme of Kafka's story *A Hunger Artist*. The title of the story may seem to us, today, a strange one but in Kafka's lifetime, that is to say in the years around the turn of the 19th century to the 20th, there were many such "hunger artists" who earned both their own living and the living of their impresarios through "performance fasting". They had themselves exhibited to the public in glass showcases or cages, on market squares or in the halls of community centres, and pursued strict fasts that often went on for weeks on end, followed closely and passionately by the entire local population. They consumed nothing but water and watchmen were employed even through the nights to testify and prove that they did not "cheat" in this regard. Admission was charged to those who wished to come and admire the athletic fasting. The local newspapers gave regular updates on these "hunger artists'" states of health and morale, day by day. Some of them even achieved country- or continent-wide fame, made European tours and enjoyed the reputation of possessing supernatural powers. At this period it was not yet known that prolonged fasting can have the effect of inducing euphoric hallucinatory states which mean that the fasting individual does not feel any pangs of hunger. The best-known "hunger artist" of this era, whom Kafka likely took as his model in this story, was Arnold Ehret. In 1909 he pursued, displayed in a glass showcase, a fast which lasted 49 days, a world record at the time. This, of course, was also a period in which cinemas, radio broadcasts, Ferris wheels and other modern attractions were first establishing themselves among the public, so that interest in this "performance fasting" as a form of mass entertainment was slowly but steadily beginning to wane.

Kafka's story takes this "end of an era" as its theme. *A Hunger Artist* was published first in a Berlin literary magazine and then became, two years later, the title piece of Kafka's final collection of short stories, which appeared shortly before his death in 1924. All four of the stories in this small collection, in fact, concern the relationship between one or another sort of "artist" and the artist's audience. They thematize the fact that artist and audience need one another while nonetheless failing to achieve mutual understanding and remaining, at bottom, strangers one to the other. The tale of the "hunger artist" who is protagonist of the title story is also a tale of misrecognition:

[...] For their elders he was often just a joke that happened to be in fashion. But the children stood open-mouthed [...] marvelling at him as he sat there pallid in black tights with his ribs sticking out

so prominently [...] down among straw on the ground [...] answering questions with a constrained smile or perhaps stretching an arm through the bars so that one might feel how thin it was [...].[31]

Like the real hunger artists just mentioned, Kafka's hunger artist too is watched over at night by watchmen employed by his impresario. Kafka throws in the disturbing detail that these watchers were "strangely enough, usually butchers". The men, however, tend to spend the nights playing cards rather than intently watching the man in the cage. Much preferred by the hunger artist himself are those rare watchmen who take their duties very seriously and observe his fasting with great punctiliousness. If, for any reason, the watchmen do indeed become distracted and look away, the hunger artist, overcoming the weakness induced by his fasting, begins loudly to sing, so as to exclude any suspicion that he might be taking advantage of this inattention to "cheat" and gulp down a little food after all.

Even this does not prevent, however, rumours from circulating in the population that that hunger artist somehow secretly takes nourishment under cover of darkness, or even bribes his watchmen to look the other way:

No one could produce first-hand

evidence that the fast had really been rigorous and continuous. Only the artist himself could know that. He was, therefore, bound to be the sole completely satisfied spectator of his own fast.[32]

But in contrast to the many charlatans active in the "performance fasting" business Kafka's hunger artist is prompted to fasting by the pure passion for fasting itself. He does not even find fasting hard:

For he alone knew, what no other initiate knew, how easy it was to fast. It was the easiest thing in the world.[33]

Were it up to him, he would go on fasting indefinitely, and he becomes more and more annoyed with his impresario, whose policy is never to allow a "hunger performance" to run for more than forty consecutive days. At the end of this period, the impresario always organizes a great public ceremony with a brass band in which two ladies chosen from the audience get to support the hunger artist as he emerges, tottering, from his cage or showcase. Two doctors check the state of his health, weigh him, and call out their results through a megaphone to the astonished crowd. Then, on each such occasion, it is the turn of the impresario to make his contribution to the performance:

The impresario came forward and [...] grasped him round the emaciated waist with exaggerated caution so that the frail condition he was in might be appreciated and committed him to the care of the

blenching ladies, not without secretly giving him a shaking so that his legs and body tottered and swayed.[34]

These ladies then accompany the hunger artist to a table at which there is gingerly administered to him his first meal.

This routine limitation of the fasting performance to forty days, however, is not motivated by any real concern for the hunger artist's wellbeing but rather by mere commercial considerations, since the impresario is aware that after forty days the interest of the paying public begins to wane. The hunger artist himself, though, is unwilling to let any such criterion stand as a reason to limit his fasting:

Why stop fasting at this particular moment? [...] Why should he be cheated of the fame he would get for fasting longer?[35]

Since, however, like all artists, he is forced to place himself in the service of the culture industry he gives, against his will, over and over again the same performance and becomes, as the years pass, ever more sad and discontented. The reason for this sadness, namely that he is never allowed to fast for more than forty days at a stretch, remains, indeed, completely hidden from his audience:

And if some good-natured person, feeling sorry for him, tried to console him by pointing out that his melancholy was probably caused by fasting,

it could happen [...] that he reacted with an outburst of fury and, to the general alarm, began to shake the bars of his cage like a wild animal.[36]

The impresario is in the habit of punishing the hunger artist for such outbursts by explaining to the public that they were to be put down to the immense strain of going without food for such long periods: a strain that well-fed people could never begin to imagine, the consequences of which had, therefore, to be forgiven him. What is more, the impresario does a good trade in images of the hunger artist lying exhausted, apparently at the very limit of his strength, on his bed on the fortieth day of every fasting performance:

This perversion of the truth, familiar to the artist though it was, always unnerved him afresh and proved too much for him.[37]

When, in addition to all this, audience numbers also begin to dwindle, the hunger artist ends his partnership with his impresario. He becomes his own manager, working in a circus which agrees to display him as a secondary attraction in a cage next to cages containing animals which also attract the public. Here, he is allowed to continue his public fasting for longer periods than forty days and, for every day that he fasts, the corresponding number is hung up on a little notice board on the front of his cage. In the pauses between the circus performances the circus audiences go to look at the animals in their cages and therefore cannot help passing the hunger artist's cage and casting a glance at him. But after a while he begins to lose his power of attraction even as a secondary entertainment during the pauses in the main show. Audiences prefer to hurry by him to reach the cages where the lions and leopards are on display. Since, unlike the circus animals, he requires, due to his indefinitely prolonged fasting, no feeding at all, the circus overseers pay less and less attention to him, until he is completely forgotten:

> [...] The little notice board telling the number of fast days achieved, which at first was changed carefully every day, had long stayed at the same figure, for after the first few weeks even this small

> task seemed pointless to the staff. And so the artist simply fasted on and on, as he had once dreamed of doing [...] But no one counted the days; no one, not even the artist himself, knew what records he was already breaking, and his heart grew heavy.[38]

The story ends with one of the circus overseers doing his rounds, believing himself to have come upon an empty cage, and wondering why this latter, being clearly still usable, has been left to stand unoccupied. Digging around in its straw with his iron rod, the overseer discovers, to his astonishment, the hunger artist, not yet dead but thin as a rake and clearly close to death:

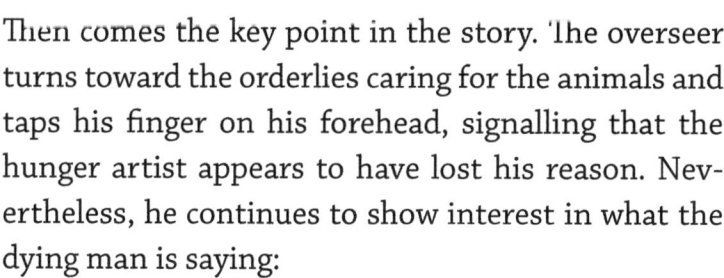

"Are you still fasting?" asked the overseer. "When on earth do you mean to stop?" "Forgive me, everybody," whispered the hunger artist [...] "I

always wanted you to admire my fasting" [...] "But you shouldn't admire it." "Well, then we don't admire it," said the overseer. "But why shouldn't we admire it?" "Because I have to fast. I can't help it," said the hunger artist.[39]

Then comes the key point in the story. The overseer turns toward the orderlies caring for the animals and taps his finger on his forehead, signalling that the hunger artist appears to have lost his reason. Nevertheless, he continues to show interest in what the dying man is saying:

"What a fellow you are," said the overseer. "And why can't you help it?" "Because," said the hunger artist [...] "I couldn't find the food I liked. If

I had found it, believe me, I should have made no fuss and stuffed myself like you or anyone else." These were his last words [...].[40]

The few concluding lines of the story which follow these last words display a striking resemblance to the concluding scene of *The Metamorphosis*. Just as the latter story ends by establishing a striking contrast between the "young body stretching in the sun" of Gregor's sister and the dusty, dried-out corpse of Gregor himself, this story ends with an equally striking displacement of the ruined and emaciated dying body of the hunger artist by the living body of a young panther:

"Well, clear this out now!" said the overseer," and they buried the hunger artist, straw and all. Into the cage

they put a young panther. Even the most insensitive felt it refreshing to see this wild creature leaping around the cage that had so long been dreary [...] The joy of life streamed with such ardent passion from his throat that for the onlookers it was not easy to stand the shock of it.[41]

As is always the case with any of Kafka's works, *A Hunger Artist* has received many different interpretations. Thus, it might be relevant that Kafka himself suffered, at certain periods of his life, from eating disorders, that he was a vegetarian, and that he had a certain sympathy with clinics that practiced various types of fasting and dieting. But above and beyond this the basic situation which Kafka describes as that of the hunger artist, namely one of a need to act in a certain way driven by some inner compulsion, might well be interpreted as a reflection of Kafka's own artistic ambitions. This would be indicated, for example, by the key passage in which the hunger artist confesses why he fasts:

"Because I have to fast. I can't help it" […].[42]

The admiration, then, which the hunger artist once received from the public, had been, it appears for him only something of secondary rank. The fact is, he had had to fast. Kafka too wrote, as he confessed elsewhere, because he had to write and could not do otherwise. Many of his stories were not intended for the public at all. It is likely that he destroyed some of what he had written. It is certain that he left instructions to his friend and executor Max Brod to destroy, unpublished, much of the writing left, at his death, among his private papers. Fortunately for posterity, Brod refused to carry out this instruction.

To sum up, then: even if its focus appears to be the self-imposed compulsion of the hunger artist to engage in prolonged fasting, this story too is, in the end, a story of the collapse of the social bond and a pointing-up of the absolute necessity, for our very existence, of the maintaining of the structure of inter-personal relationships. Even during the period of his success no acknowledgment is accorded to the real personal ambitions and motivations behind the hunger artist's "hunger performances". This is all the more the case once he has confessed that he has no choice but to forgo eating. At this point, he is even stigmatized as mentally ill.

Rather than some attempt being made to communicate with him, judgment is simply passed on him. Be it the audience tacitly supposing that he must be committing some sort of fraud as regards the length of his fasts and refusing to acknowledge his personal honesty, or the impresario falsely explaining the artist's fits of rage over being forced to cut short his fasting as if it were a consequence of the fasting itself, the hunger artist finds himself in both these cases pushed into the position of a mere object, gaped at and judged.

But what costs, in the end, the hunger artist his life is not the lack of acknowledgment of his art and its dismissal as fraud or mental illness but rather the fact that his life lacks, throughout, any and every form of human empathy and commiseration. He is "forgotten", not just as an artist but as a human being.

The Trial :
Accused, But Why and By Whom?

One of the three uncompleted novels which Kafka has left to us also begins with a sentence which has become legendary in modern literary history:

Someone must have been telling tales about Josef K. for one morning, without having done anything wrong, he was arrested.[43]

The entire novel, in fact, turns around the increasingly hopeless situation of the bank employee Josef K. who, at the age of thirty, suddenly finds himself indicted by some mysterious legal or governmental authority and driven into ever narrower straits. The questions he poses as to who is accusing him, and even as to what exactly he is accused of, all go unanswered. The tale begins with the sudden intrusion of three black-clad men into K.'s apartment. These men announce themselves as "guards" and inform K. that he is under arrest. K. is at first completely baffled as to what is going on:

What kind of people were they? [...] Which department did they belong to? After all, K. had rights; the country was at peace; the laws had not been suspended – who, then, had the audacity to descend on him in the privacy of his own home?[44]

K. rapidly seeks out the papers proving his identity and thrusts them into the faces of these self-proclaimed "guards", saying:

"Here is my identification. Now show me yours and, above all, your warrant." "Good Lord," said the guard, "Why can't you just accept the situation instead of pointlessly insisting on trying to annoy us? Do you think you can bring your damned trial to a rapid conclusion by arguing with us guards about identity and warrants? We're

minor officials [...] but we're still able to understand that, before they order such an arrest the authorities in whose employment we are will go into the reasons for the arrest and the particulars of the person to be arrested. There is no mistake."[45]

This claim that no written legitimation is necessary because there can be no question of a mistake's having been made only serves to provoke K. even more, since he really is unaware of having ever done anything wrong. When he begins to curse at the guards and suggests that the whole incident might just be a bad joke that someone is playing on him, the guard asks him in a very serious tone whether he could possibly really think that this is all just a joke. K. makes a certain concession here:

"[...] I'm not saying it's a joke." "Quite right," said the supervisor [...] "On the other hand, however," K. went on, [...] "the matter cannot be that important [...] Which of the authorities is conducting the proceedings? Are you a state official? None of you is in uniform [...]"[46]

The supervisor retorts that it is not his place to pass judgment about the clothes worn by the guards. If he continues in this manner, he tells K., things are likely only to get worse for him.

"Think less about us and [...] more about yourself instead. And don't go on about your feeling of innocence so much [...]"[47]

Despite this "arrest", however, Josef K. is finally allowed to leave his house and go to work. The "guards" withdraw. Some days later K. receives a phone call saying that he is to attend a preliminary hearing on the following Sunday. The hearing, oddly, is to be held not in any of the central law-court buildings but rather in a backstreet in one of the poorer areas on the edge of the city. Neither an exact time for the hearing nor an exact room-number is given to him. When he arrives at the address in question he finds that he has to make his way through a labyrinth of halls and corridors until he finally finds the place where the hearing is being held. A large number of people are already gathered in the room. At a writing desk at its far end sits someone who appears to be the examining magistrate. This much might at least be assumed from the fact that he reprimands K. for being late and then goes on to ask him to confirm that he is a painter and decorator. K. reacts to this with derision, replying:

"Your question, sir, as to whether I am a painter and decorator [...] is entirely typical of the proceedings which are being taken against me."[48]

He takes this confusion as to his identity as an apt point of departure for a passionate speech in which he describes in detail and at length his entirely unjustified arrest and the initiation of legal proceedings against him apparently without formal written accusation. He hopes with this speech to awaken the righteous indignation of the many people assembled in the hearing room and to draw them onto his side, making clear to them that he has been the victim of untransparent machinations and that the same danger constantly threatens every other citizen as well:

"There is no doubt that there is a large organization at work behind this court's every operation, in my case the arrest and today's examination. An organization with a [...] numerous entourage of ushers, clerks and perhaps even, I do not hesitate to use the word,

executioners. And the point of this large organization, gentlemen? It consists in arresting innocent persons and instituting pointless and mostly, as in my case, fruitless proceedings against them."[49]

Whereas, at the beginning of this speech, K. had seemed to pick up, here and there, a sign or two of sympathy and concurral from the people assembled in the room, he is surprised to be met, at the end, only with total silence. He now begins to examine more closely the serious faces of the black-clad men around him and makes a terrible discovery:

They all had (the same) badges, as far as could be seen. The groups on the right and the left, that had looked like two parties, all belonged together and he saw, as he suddenly swung round, the same badges on the collar of the examining magistrate [...].[50]

Suddenly, K. understands everything. This session he had been summoned to had not, after all, been the public hearing that he had taken it to be. He had never, even at the beginning, had any real chance of convincing these people of his innocence. If there had been some laughter, and some apparent concurral from the crowd, at the beginning, all this had been intended only to draw him out:

"So!" cried K., throwing his arms into the air – this sudden insight needed space – "You're all officials, as I see; you're the corrupt gang I was inveighing against."[51]

With this, K. rushes from the room where this "corrupt gang" is assembled. With the help of his uncle he secures himself a lawyer. When K. and his uncle go to consult him, however, the lawyer is lying sick in bed and he introduces both of them to a young woman named Leni, who appears to be both nurse and legal assistant. While K.'s uncle speaks with the lawyer about this strange accusation, Leni lures K. into an adjoining room, where she promises to personally aid and accompany him through his trial. This promise, however, openly takes the form of a seduction, with Leni seating herself on K.'s lap as she speaks to him. K. declares himself willing to accept her help but expresses a feat that erotic adventures like this might distract him from bringing his trial to a successful conclusion:

"That's not the mistake you're making," said Leni. "You're too intransigent. That's what I've heard. "Who said that?" asked K. He could feel her body against his chest and was looking down at her thick, dark, firmly plaited hair. "It would be giving away too much if I told

you that, "Leni replied. "Please don't ask me for names but stop making this mistake [...] No one can resist this court. You just have to confess [...] It's only then that

there's a possibility of escaping, only then – though even that's not possible without outside help. But you needn't worry about that. I'll provide the help myself."[52]

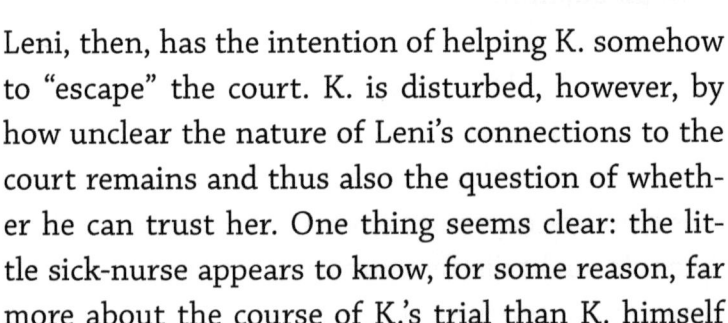

Leni, then, has the intention of helping K. somehow to "escape" the court. K. is disturbed, however, by how unclear the nature of Leni's connections to the court remains and thus also the question of whether he can trust her. One thing seems clear: the little sick-nurse appears to know, for some reason, far more about the course of K.'s trial than K. himself does. K. cannot do, however, what Leni asks of him, namely "escape" by making a confession, because he has no idea what crime it is that he has to confess. Besides to Leni, K. also enters into love relationships with two other women, one of them the wife of a court official. These women also declare that they want to help K. to avoid conviction and condemnation. But in these cases too K. must, naturally, be apprehensive that the women might really, all along, be working for the other side. When the legal submission prepared by the lawyer whom K. has engaged fails to progress through the court system, since he is allowed no insight into the relevant court files and finds it difficult to formulate an effective submission relative to charges he can form no clear idea of, K. decides to dispense with his services. At the same time he ends his affair with the lawyer's ambiguous assistant Leni. He becomes increasingly mistrustful:

Was it the trial that threw him this way and that, so that he could no longer tell who was his friend, who his enemy?[53]

K. retreats further and further into isolation because he no longer knows whom he can trust. On a visit to a church he seems for a moment to find support in a priest whom he encounters there who, astonishingly, proves to be aware of the proceedings against K. and even admits that he "belongs to the court himself". K. hopes through this priest to finally gain some clarity about his own experience with the court and confesses to him how worried he is becoming about his trial's outcome:

„"I used to think that it would turn out all right," said K., "Now I sometimes even doubt that myself [...] Do you know?" "No," said the priest. "But I fear it will end badly. At least for the moment, they think your

guilt is proven [...]". "But I'm not guilty," said K. "How can a person be guilty, anyway? We're all human, every single one of us." "That is correct," said the priest. "But that is the way guilty people talk."[54]

But instead of giving him further advice the priest now recounts to K. a kind of parable about a "man from the country" who is searching finally to find out the truth about guilt and innocence. The parable speaks of this man arriving, in the course of his search, "before the Law", "the Law" being conceived of here as a kind of hall from whose entrance "there streams an inextinguishable radiance." Before this entrance stands a doorkeeper. The "man from the country" approaches this doorkeeper and "asks to be allowed into the Law". The doorkeeper, however, refuses him entrance, giving him only a stool to sit and wait on. "There," continues the priest,

"He sits for days and years [...] Before he dies, all the things he has experienced during the whole time merge in his mind into a question he has not yet put to the doorkeeper [...] namely: 'How is it that in all these years

no one apart from me has asked to be let in (to the Law)?' The doorkeeper realizes that the man is nearing his end and so, in order to be audible to his fading hearing, he bellows at him:

'No one else could be granted entry here, because this entrance was intended for you alone. I shall now go and shut it.'"[55]

K., however, fails to understand the meaning of the parable recounted to him by the priest. What can any of that have to do with him? Is the meaning that he too is to be kept waiting, like "the man from the country"? Or is it rather that he, like this man, has let slip by him his only chance of achieving clarity by accepting, due to a lack of courage to do otherwise, that he, like others, had simply to wait patiently for the outcome of his trial? Only one thing is certain: that, for the "man from the country" in the parable, the door to knowledge remains forever closed. K. too proves unable to acquire any insight or understanding regarding what is going on. Finally, Kafka tells us of how, on the eve of his thirty-first birthday, at nine o'clock in the evening, he is visited once again by two black-clad men:

"So you're the ones who've come for me?" he asked. The men nodded [...] He went over to the window and looked out into the dark street once more."[56]

The two men, whom he clearly understands to be his executioners, lead him, in order to carry out the sentence of death passed on him, to a little stone quarry on the edge of the city. They lay him down on one of the stones and take out a large butcher's knife. K. has to watch as they spend long minutes checking the edges of the blade:

Where was the judge he had never seen? [...] He raised his hands and splayed his fingers. But the hands of one of the men were placed on K.'s throat, whilst the other plunged the knife into his heart and turned it round twice.[57]

With his sight and life fading away, K. manages to formulate one final sentence, on which the novel ends:

"Like a dog!" he said. It seemed as if his shame would live on after him.[58]

K. dies, then, "like a dog". And indeed, it is the case that he is slaughtered like an animal, without any explanation of what is being done. Kafka exposes here, so to speak, his readers to the same condition of total ignorance and powerlessness as K. himself is exposed to. Right up until the very end of the novel it remains entirely unclear to us just what K. is on trial for, and who it is that has indicted him. It is left up to each individual reader to try to make sense of the events recounted.

Needless to say, the first interpretation of this story which suggests itself is the sociological or political one, whereby *The Trial* is a terribly accurate anticipation of the complete disregard for human dignity which was to become general in the totalitarian societies established in Europe and elsewhere after Kafka's death. The "raid"-like arrest of K., for example, by men who wear no recognizable uniform but rather just black coats, who provide no proof of their identity and who, in the end, return to summarily liquidate the arrested party, clearly uncannily anticipate certain practices later used by the Gestapo.

Likewise, K.'s discovery that the people assembled in the hall in which his first "preliminary hearing" is held all in fact wear the same insignia, and that they are letting themselves be directed, moreover, by certain subtle hand-signals of the judge's, can easily be seen as foreshadowing the process of *Gleichschaltung*, or "total coordination", to which the Nazis and other fascist regimes subjected their societies once they had seized power. Finally, we might see a remarkably accurate "pre-portrait" of the vast system of informants and complex social surveillance that characterized the dictatorships of the middle decades of the 20th century in the experiences that lead K. eventually to think that he cannot trust or place confidence in anyone, since every person he encounters may be a spy of the court system, or a collaborator within it.

The Trial, then, can be considered as, at least under one of its most significant aspects, a prophecy as uncanny as Nostradamus's of the catastrophe that was about to befall the century in which Kafka lived his adult life. Kafka wrote *The Trial* in 1915, that is to say, almost twenty years before Hitler's seizure of power in Germany. He was, indeed, a personal witness to the nationalistic mood that seized Germany and the German-speaking region of the Austro-Hungarian empire in which he lived after the outbreak of the First World War, even if this was a mood which, in contrast to many of his contemporaries, he never shared. Kafka could also hardly have failed to note the growing hostility between the Czech, German and Jewish populations in his native city of Prague. But these tensions developing in Kafka's lifetime within the Austro-Hungarian Empire were not such as could really have permitted anyone to foresee those totalitarian practices, even up to the point of brutal liquidation, the surreal mirror-image of which Kafka provides in *The Trial*.

When Max Brod, Kafka's close friend and executor of his will, was giving a public talk in the city of Wiesbaden in 1927, some three years after Kafka's death, a young student in the audience rose and interjected: "Do you know that one day our century will be called 'the century of Kafka'"?"[59] This interjection was certainly justified, since there is no denying that we see in Kafka's stories a remarkable prefiguring of the stripping of all rights and reduction to powerlessness of human beings in the totalitarian societies that were just then beginning to take hold. If philosophers such as Theodor Adorno and Hannah Arendt were to speak in philosophical terms, somewhat later, of alienation and of the anonymous domination of bureaucracy, Kafka had already long since provided the concrete details that fill out these philosophical accounts. *The Trial* continues, even a century on, to be seen as one of the key texts of the 20th century.

So much, then, for *The Trial*'s political interpretation. But as gripping a feature of the novel as its prescience with regard to imminent historical developments are its phenomenological discoveries with regard to the dynamics of interpersonal relations. When one considers *The Trial* from this perspective what strikes one is that, at the beginning of the story, K. strongly resists the persecution he is subjected to, vehemently insists on the principle "innocent until proven guilty", and maintains a firm belief in himself. He makes, at one point, a passionate speech against the abuse of law and the arbitrary rule of the authorities and is so pro-active as to seek out the help of a lawyer. But as experience teaches him more and more that no one is supporting him or standing by him in this resistance and that, on the contrary, he is constantly urged by everyone to confess his guilt, to accept the validity of the trial and of the approaching judgment, then he begins to lose all the belief in himself that he had at first succeeded in retaining and he is cast into insecurity. This insecurity increases still farther when he learns that, whatever he does, he is sure in any case to be condemned in the end. He hears at one point of people known to his lawyer who are said to be able to read off from the shape of a person's lips whether they will be found guilty or not:

"Going from your lips, those people maintained that you would definitely, and soon, be condemned" […] "My lips?" asked K., taking out a pocket mirror and looking at himself. "I can't see anything special about my lips" […].[60]

But even if this is the case, K.'s self-confidence is seriously shaken by this remark. The trial, accepted by everyone except himself and proceeding steadily without need of any action or intervention from his side, hovers over him like a sword of Damocles. Due to the sense of insecurity maintained in him by the constantly threatening guilty verdict K. gradually loses everything: his job at the bank, his will and courage to live, and all his social contacts:

> Was it the trial that threw him this way and that, so that he could no longer tell who was his friend, who his enemy? [61]

But why had K. not at least tried to resist when his executioners came and fetched him in his apartment? The answer is simple. His interpersonal reality had already acquired a "no way out" dimension and it was this interpersonal reality that blocked all action on his part. He had by then already been, for so many months, "declared dead" by the world that he had internalized this fate and accepts his death as a fait accompli. At the beginning of the execution in the quarry on the edge of town K. sees the window of a house in the distance fly open and a human figure lean out, stretching its arms toward him. For a moment, he allows himself to hope for some aid or intervention, for "objections he'd forgotten" that might still, even now, bring about a turn in the process of trial and condemnation. But already a moment later he recognizes that the judgment will inevitably be executed, in accordance with a long-fixed plan.

What happens to K. can happen to us all. We are, each of us, dependent on the judgments of other human beings because we create our respective realities never alone, just by and through ourselves, but in a constant process of exchange with others. If everyone agrees that the grass is green, then it is green. If everyone says that this man or that man is guilty, then he is guilty. We are, to a significant extent, always delivered into the power of others. Most people will not, indeed, immediately lose their moral balance and their hold on their own existence as soon as somebody else insults them or, as Kafka describes K.'s case at the start of *The Trial*, "tells tales" about them. But when the "tale-tellers" begin to amount to large numbers of people, and people whose opinions matter to us, keeping one's balance becomes significantly more difficult. Finally, when, as in K.'s case, absolutely everyone around him judges that he will and must be found guilty, this judgment acquires an irreversible, irrecusable dynamic of its own:

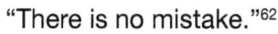

"There is no mistake."[62]

K. surrenders, in the end, to social reality. He knows that the judgment, even though it is plainly unjust and unfounded, will in the end be executed upon him. Grotesquely, however, he is still so much a part of this society that is executing him that he feels shame over the particular manner of the execution. It is, he feels, an execution unworthy of a human being and resembles rather the butchering of an animal on the butcher's block than the carrying out of a judgment handed down by official authorities. The tragically sarcastic "punch line" of Kafka's story, then, is that the modern human being still feels himself in death, and even beyond death, obligated to that very society whose victim he has become:

"Like a dog!" he said. It seemed as if his shame would live on after him.[63]

77

To sum up, then: "Tales are told" about the bank employee K. and a mysterious trial mounted against him. In the course of time he succumbs to a dynamic of shame-inducing "othering", since he has clearly been singled out from all those around him as "the man accused". The people in his immediate social circle, and even certain third parties hitherto unknown to him, are all aware that he is "on trial". But more than this: all these people, both acquaintances and total strangers, treat the trial that he is being subjected to as something that could not be otherwise. K. finds himself less and less able, as time passes, to distance himself from this intersubjective truth. After some initial resistance he comes himself to feel, and thereby internalizes, the inevitability of his condemnation. It is for this reason that he complies, in the end, almost without resistance with the instructions of his executioners and dies also physically his "social death".

The Judgment –
Who Doesn't "Measure Up" Has No Right to Be At All

Georg Bendemann, the protagonist of Kafka's story *The Judgment*, is, like so many of Kafka's leading
characters, a young successful businessman. As the
story opens, Georg appears to be in a good position
in life and is especially content because he is about
to get married. We find him writing a letter to an
old friend who has emigrated to Russia in order to
inform him of this, his approaching wedding. We
learn that Georg has, up to this point, omitted any
mention to his friend of the imminent happy event
and indeed of the success he has been enjoying in his
business, since the friend in question has, in recent
years, himself known very little happiness or good
luck either in his professional or in his private life.
On the urging of his fiancée, however, and hoping,
for his own part, that his "good friend" will be able to
put aside his own misery and share in his joy, Georg
is sitting down this sunny morning and writing to
him after all. Before sending off his letter to Saint
Petersburg, however, he decides to seek the advice of
his aged, bedridden father. But when Georg explains
to him his intention the old man gives a shocking,

brutal response:

"You have no friend in Saint Petersburg."[64]

He follows this up with a whole series of disturbing, barely credible statements. Suddenly changing his tune, he says that he is very well acquainted with Georg's friend in Saint Petersburg but that this friend has long since turned away from Georg. Fulfilling his duty as a father, the old man claims, he has been maintaining a steady correspondence himself with the man whom Georg is talking about and has long preceded Georg in informing him about the coming marriage, Georg's taking over of the family business and also, the father goes on, about all the acts of dishonesty that Georg had committed both in these business and in other matters:

"Of course I know your friend. He would have been a son after my own heart. That's why you've been playing him false all these years. Why else?"[65]

Georg, uncannily and inexplicably, suddenly finds himself experiencing genuine terror at this "bogey" conjured up by his father, as if the wild, incoherent claims being made by the old man really did correspond to some deeper truth. This image of his friend as someone with whom his father has been maintaining an intensive correspondence and who is far dearer to his father than he could ever be himself "touches his imagination as never before". But this is not all. The father, who had up to this point seemed so unthreatening in his age and frailty, now begins to cast at Georg, still in his nightshirt but rising from a lying to a standing position on the bed, a series of deeply wounding, even shattering charges and accusations: Georg, claims the father, has pushed him out of the business that he, the father, had built up, locked him away in a back room, and was now, to put the capper on it, about to get married to a woman whom the father, shockingly, describes in terms of the lowest crudity and vulgarity:

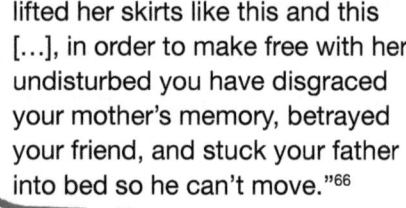

"Because she lifted up her skirts," his father began to flute, "because she lifted up her skirts like this, the nasty creature," and, mimicking her, he lifted his nightshirt so high that one could see the scar on his thigh from his war wound, "because she

lifted her skirts like this and this […], in order to make free with her undisturbed you have disgraced your mother's memory, betrayed your friend, and stuck your father into bed so he can't move."[66]

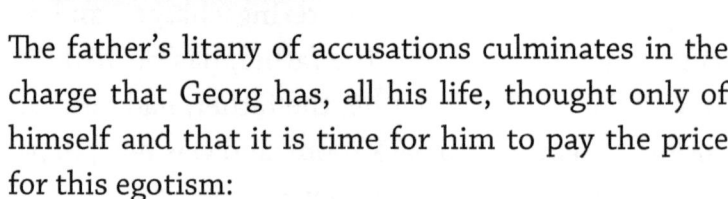

The father's litany of accusations culminates in the charge that Georg has, all his life, thought only of himself and that it is time for him to pay the price for this egotism:

"So now you know what else there was in the world besides yourself, till now you've known only about yourself. An innocent child, yes, that you were, truly. But still more truly have you been a devilish human being! – and therefore take note! I sentence you now to death by drowning!"[67]

Georg is shaken by this judgment to the very core of his being, because it is a judgment that is open to no interpretation or discussion. He simply hears it and accepts it, without even the least doubt arising in him regarding its legitimacy or justification. In his inmost being he feels that it is indeed the case that he has forfeited his right to life and is bound now, indeed, to throw himself in the river and drown. He rushes out of the house toward the great bridge over this river:

Out of the front door he rushed, driven toward the water. Already he was grasping at the railings as a starving man clutches food. He swung himself over [...], called in a low voice: "Dear parents, I have always loved you, all the same", and let himself drop. At this moment an unending stream of traffic was just going over the bridge.[68]

The story *The Judgment* ends with these words. Max Brod and certain other interpreters have proposed a reading of the tale that runs quite counter to first impressions. They see in Georg's apparently panicky rush from the house and his swinging himself over the railings of the bridge not a tragic suicide but, on the contrary, the son's final success in freeing himself from the bonds of his parental home and his entry into a life of his own determination. Brod points out that, in terms of the actual letter of the text, the end of *The Judgment* contains no indication that Georg's leaping from the bridge into the water leads to him actually drowning. The waters of the river, Brod suggests, might be a metaphor. Ever since earliest times, the river has been a place of baptism, purification and rebirth. One can, then, and even must, says Brod, read *The Judgment* as the story of an emancipation.

Brod's, however, is only one among the more than two hundred analyses of this story propped up by one sort of literary theory or another. *The Judgment*, indeed, may be the most analyzed and interpreted work in the whole of German-language literature. Only one thing unites just about every one of the many different interpretations: Kafka surely thematized, in the rapidly escalating father-son conflict which he portrays in this story, his own problematical relationship with his father. This is confirmed by the remark which Kafka confides to his diary early in 1913 when correcting the proofs, prior to publication, of this story composed in a single night in the autumn of the previous year:

[...] The story came out of me like a real birth, covered with filth and slime [...].[69]

One feels all the more disinclined, then, to add to the already numerous psychoanalytical, hermeneutic, and discourse-analytical interpretations yet another, philosophical one. But the thesis I advance here, namely that Kafka describes immanently within his work the essence of interpersonal relations, is really not a further, added interpretation but only the simple recognition of something that is clearly the case. And on this core substance of "what is the case" in the story the speculative question of whether, after the story's end, Georg drowns in the river or not has no effect. The central idea of the story has already been enunciated in terms which could hardly have been clearer:

The son, in other words, is declared by the father to be "dead to him", and thereby to the entire social and human world, much as Gregor Samsa is, by his father, in *The Metamorphosis*. This "death sentence" is in fact just the culmination of a long process of withdrawal of all paternal acknowledgment which has run through the story from its beginning to its very end. The father denigrates all that the son has achieved in business, declares the commercially unsuccessful friend of Georg's in Russia to be a "son after his own heart" far dearer to him than his actual son, denounces Georg's sensitivity toward this friend's feelings as mere cowardice and, finally, speaks of Georg's fiancée in terms of the lowest crudity and brutality, portraying the engagement as a scandal for the family. The whole story, in short, turns in essence around the refusal of recognition to the son in every area of his existence.

The point of the story, however, is not just the refusal of any benevolent recognition but rather the reversal of this benevolent recognition into the radical accusation of having been a moral failure, an egotistical and "wicked" human being. It is this "judgment" that eventually pulls the rug out from under Georg's existence, so that he becomes his own executioner.

Just like the protagonist of this story, Georg Bendemann, Kafka himself had serious problems gaining the recognition and acknowledgment of his own father. The portrait of this latter that Kafka has handed down to us is one of a man of very little culture or education but great vitality and strength of will who had worked his way up from poverty into the position of a successful businessman with highly aggressive and autocratic traits. In a long personal letter to his father, which Kafka, characteristically, never sent off, and which has came to be read and perceived as something like another of his literary fictions (Kafka's *Letter to the Father* is often spoken of in the same breath as *The Trial* or *The Judgment*) Kafka criticizes his father's authoritarian methods of education:

> You can only treat a child in the way you yourself are constituted, with vigour, noise and hot temper, and in this case this seemed to you, into the bargain, extremely suitable, because you wanted to bring me up to be a strong, brave boy.[71]

Kafka's father had absolutely no time or respect for his son's literary ambitions. His mind was focussed rather, obsessively, on his constantly growing business, whose many employees he treated with the same brutality as he did his family, calling them "dogs" and "paid enemies".[72] Kafka had been particularly horrified to hear his father say of one of his assistants, who suffered from tuberculosis:

"The sooner he dies the better, the mangy dog."[73]

Farther on in this famous *Letter to the Father* we find Kafka writing:

[...] You had as terrible an effect on these people as on me.[74]

IIis father, Kafka tells us, had begun very early to reproach him with having "no head for business", tending to get lost in "pipe dreams" and, finally, with simply being a weakling. "It's bound to end badly with you", the father would constantly repeat. The consequences of this style of education were, as Kafka puts it, that:

My peculiarity was not accorded any recognition; but since I felt it, I could not fail to recognize a [...] condemnation.[75]

Kafka, then, very much shared with his protagonist Georg Bendemann the feeling of being "condemned" by his own father. There can be no doubt but that Kafka, in the story *The Judgment*, is once again conveying to us a very simple truth. If we are not recognized in our inner reality and authenticity and if, in particular, some person whose judgment matters greatly to us refuses us, for a long or even just a short period, their acknowledgment, this can lead to an impairment of our own sense of self-worth and, in extreme cases like that of Georg Bendemann, to a loss of all sense of even the right to exist, and thus of the will to live.

Kafka's Central Idea: The Structure of Interpersonal Relations

Kafka is an author of literary works, not a philosopher. His central idea, nonetheless, is a deeply philosophical one. With incomparable acuity he succeeds in pointing up for us the basic ontological structure of human interpersonal relationships. The word "ontology" is composed by joining together the Ancient Greek terms on, which means "existent thing" and logos, which means "doctrine". "Ontology", then, means "the doctrine of what exists and what does not exist" and thus concerns, among other structures, those basic structures that human inter-relations have to conform to in order for these inter-relations to exist at all.

Kafka's entire body of work is, throughout, a pointing-up of the inescapable ontological structures defining relations between human beings.[76] He makes it very clear what a human being needs to live, what we lack, and what tends to threaten us existentially when it is withheld from us. Man does not live by bread alone. He is rather radically dependent on other people's wanting him, acknowledging him, assigning or ascribing, as it were, being to him. This, of course, is quite especially true for infants and children. But even much later in life there continues to exist an invisible bond between an adult individual's own existence and that of other such individuals.

Kafka, in his stories, shows us in the most gripping way just what this bond which links human beings together on a deeper level consists in. His "heroes", are, in all his stories and novels, young, successful men who, initially, are earning good livings as commercial travellers, helmsmen, bank employees, hunger artists or businessmen but who have, as it were, the carpet of existence pulled out from under their feet by some "excommunication" which, though subtle, sometimes takes the most radical form. The reason for this is, in each case, the experience of a fundamental non-recognition of the "hero"'s person, a monstrosity of inter-personal relationship which, in most of Kafka's stories, leads to the protagonist's death.

In real life, of course, in contrast to the life of Kafka's figures, we neither physically expire nor find ourselves transformed into a beetle when our fellow men avoid us, refuse to acknowledge us or declare us "dead to them". Many people, in fact, in the real world prove to possess a core of personal identity that is astoundingly tough and resilient and that allows them to handle lack of recognition, rejection, and even threats of death without "cracking". At the very least we may say that some people are better able to handle these things than others.

For all that, however, Kafka produces, in his body of literary work, a philosophical-anthropological statement which applies, at least on the "structural" level, to all human beings. No one is capable of making him- or herself, their whole life long, independent of everyone else and living by their own resources alone. Even the legendary "hermit", who is celebrated as living a life in which he is completely "sufficient unto himself", will in fact always have developed this "self", upon which he is now able to fall back, in some living interaction and community with other human beings. No child was ever actually "raised by wolves" and research has revealed that even those recorded "strangers to human society" like Kaspar Hauser did not in fact grow up in the total isolation they were purported to have grown up in. There applies to all human beings the basic truth: no one can be his own sun.

Kafka, in his stories, reveals to us this truth in an especially pitiless light. That is to say, he illuminates the essential structure of human inter-personal relations from the perspective of those who are forced to exist in a deficient mode of these relations, i.e. in a state of a lack of recognition. For all that, though, we find in all of Kafka's stories a hidden philosophical reference to the essential relationality which belongs to the very substance of what it is to be human:

They are tied together by ropes [...][77]

Kafka, however, does not attempt to address this issue in the form of a theory of inter-personal relations that might be formulated and expounded in clear logical terms. Sartre and certain other philosophers have made the attempt to do this but have proven unable, in the end, to penetrate to the core of the mystery of human inter-relation. This sphere of the inter-human has proven, indeed, quite generally to be an extremely difficult theme for the so-called "philosophy of the subject" to address, to such a point that addressing it has almost amounted to breaching a "taboo". For this classical form of the "philosophy of the subject" the "inter-subjective", or "inter-human", sphere really has no acknowledged existence at all. If, as this classic "subject philosophy" maintains, nothing exists in the world except isolated individuals who approach other isolated individuals and acquire, by means of their cognitive and analytical apparatus, knowledge of these latter, then if any truth can be ascertained regarding the phenomenon of inter-human relation, it can be so only within the isolated consciousness of one or another of the various single individuals involved. Such essentially "de-isolating" phenomena as love, recognition, or the refusal of recognition, however, must necessarily evade full comprehension in these logical, theoretical terms.

The very reason, however, why Kafka was able to penetrate so deep into the structure of inter-human relations was because, as a literary writer, he could uninhibitedly follow out all the nuances and shadowy details of human existence, even where these surpassed and defeated logic:

I went over the wishes that I wanted to realize in life. I found that the most important [...] was the wish to attain a view of life [...] in which life, while still retaining its natural full-bodied rise and fall, would simultaneously be recognized no less clearly as a nothing, a dream, a dim hovering.[78]

It was, however, in Kafka's view, not just writers such as himself who cherished this wish to look upon life as a dream, a hovering, a mere mood. The normal human being too, Kafka suggests, tends, in the decisive moments of his or her life, to surpass and overcome logic and to behave in ways no longer comprehensible to reason:

Logic may be unshakeable, but it cannot hold out against a human being who wants to live.[79]

Kafka presents to us, from ever new angles, the struggles of his protagonists simply to live. He acquaints us with the cares and problems of these protagonists: cares and problems which, considered from a purely logical point of view, they ought really not to have and which, therefore, cannot be solved by logic or by reason. In *The Metamorphosis* we see a human being struggling with the consequences, ultimately fatal, of his transformation into a giant beetle: a transformation which is completely insusceptible of any logical explanation, indeed downright impossible. In *The Helmsman* there suddenly appears from nowhere, in a manner once again insusceptible of any logical explanation, a complete stranger on the deck of a ship in mid-ocean and pushes the story's protagonist away from the wheel at which he has served for many years, without any of his equally long-serving crewmates defending him or even appearing to miss his absence from his usual place. In *A Hunger Artist* we see a performer at one time celebrated all over his country and continent fall into such complete neglect and oblivion that he is almost swept out with the straw. In *The Trial* we see a man who has been told that he is under accusation running wildly from pillar to post failing repeatedly to find any rational explanation either of what he is accused of or of who has accused him – without this inexplicability altering the fact that he is taken out, in the end, and put to death. Finally, in *The Judgment*, we see a son react in what appears to be a completely irrationally disproportionate way to a "death sentence" passed upon him by a father who utters it in a context unsupported by any rationally comprehensible structure or authority.

Precisely, however, inasmuch as Kafka refuses, in his stories, to abide by the routines and conventions of events as we actually experience them from day to day, but rather creates an alternative landscape of dream-like sequences, moods and feelings, he carries us into a world in which our own minds can also for their part no longer cling to rules and rational agreements:

The spirit only becomes free at the point where it ceases to be invoked as a support.[80]

Kafka's key philosophical idea, then, does not arise out of any rational theory which one might be able, as one would with the theses advanced by philosophical authors, to check for its logical consistency. Rather, he leads us away into a dreamworld which is both strange and familiar to us at once. Strange, because a sudden transformation into a beetle, or a long, reasonless persecution by some anonymous authority appear to us bizarre and unusual events; but familiar too, because the sense of powerlessness and of a universal rejection is something we have all had real experience of, if not in our real lives then at least in our dreams. We also all know something of the inner struggle to find ways of avoiding such excommunication and condemnation by those around us. Kafka, then, presents no logical theory of human relations; but he makes it easier to experience the essential "relationality" of our human existence.

There can be no doubt, then, but that Kafka's writings represent phenomenological approaches to a repressed reality which we, nonetheless, all of us experience daily in our highly fragile world. And the epicentre of this fragility, argues Kafka, consists in our relations to our fellow men and women, since these relations can at any moment prove to be inadequate, unknowing or even threatening.

But of what use is this discovery to us today? Can one really conclude something, from the fictional narratives of Kafka, about the ontological structure of inter-human relationships that lies behind them? In what exactly does this structure consist? Can the "Kafkaesque" somehow be helpful to us in the end?

Of What Use Is Kafka's Discovery for Us Today?

Excommunication and "Social Death" in Kafka, in Anthropology, and in Modern Society

If one had to sum up the core idea behind Kafka's *Metamorphosis* in a single sentence, this sentence might run: turn into a beetle and you're dead. But the reason for Gregor Samsa's releasing his hold on life is not the actual physical transformation into an insect but rather the reaction of his family to this physical transformation. When he loses his job, and thus his function as breadwinner, he also loses all recognition and even affection. And not only this: in the course of the story it becomes ever clearer that Gregor was never really loved even prior to his transformation. Significantly, Kafka, who worked for fourteen years as an employee in a large insurance company, wrote in another of his stories that:

> [...] however hard one works, one does not thereby acquire a claim to be treated by everyone with love [...].[81]

After his transformation Kafka's protagonist Gregor Samsa is at first coldly "tolerated" by his family but then locked away, excommunicated, and finally "declared socially dead". When he hears his sister playing the violin a little hope reawakens in him. He emerges from his room in order to be closer to her. But she feels only horror at his approach and urges her father to some decisive action:

> "It has to go [...] That is the only way, father."[82]

It is these words of his sister's, in the last analysis, that really form Gregor's death sentence. Such sufferings as the rotting apple imbedded in his back had already, indeed, contributed to weakening him. But until this point he had still had some faint hope of recovery. But once these words declaring him already "dead to" his own family are uttered, his fate is irreversibly sealed. The consequence of this, however, is not, as one might have expected, that he becomes angry, or even that he lapses, due to the brutal withdrawal of affection by those once closest to him, into a sterile self-pity. On the contrary, his sister's statement that "it", that he himself, "has to go" appears to Gregor to be more than justified:

His own opinion that he should vanish was, if anything, even more determined than his sister's.[83]

The protagonist of *The Judgment* likewise reacts not with aggression but rather with understanding when his father suddenly, surreally condemns him to death by drowning. He opposes no resistance to this judgment at all:

> Out of the front door he rushed, driven toward the water. As he let go of the railings (he) called in a low voice: "Dear parents, I have always loved you, all the same".[84]

This internalization of the sentiment and saying "you are dead to me", taken here to the point where the person it's said about recognizes that he really must die, is in fact not just a fictive over-dramatization of Kafka's. Anthropologists and medical ethnologists speak, in this connection, of the phenomenon of "psychogenic death" or "social death".[85]

This phenomenon is still observed today in primitive peoples barely touched by modern civilization: for example, in certain regions of Equatorial, Southern and West Saharan Africa, New Guinea, Southern Australia, and Samoa. If a member of the tribe, due to the breaching of some taboo such as the ban on incest for example, has a "death curse" put on him, then he often goes into decline and dies after a few days, without any specific cause of death being discernible. Such an individual, indeed, is, once the "curse" has been put on him, ostracised and isolated by the other members of the tribe. Since, then, as has been observed by doctors and other researchers, such people continue nonetheless to take nourishment, the conclusion generally come to is that they die as a result of being unable to bear the mental pressure thereby put on them. The rituals which accompany this "death magic", for example the use of fetishes in voodoo cults, are different in different cultures and races. Common to all of them, however, is the fact that the individual "cursed", once he knows and accepts that he is "dead to" his community, does in fact soon die.

The famous French anthropologist Claude Lévi-Strauss describes this phenomenon in the following way: "An individual who is aware that he is the object of sorcery is thoroughly aware that he is doomed according to the most solemn traditions of his group. His friends and relatives share this certainty. From then on, the community withdraws. Standing aloof from the accursed, it treats him not only as if he were already dead but as if he were a source of danger for the whole group. On every occasion and by every action, the social group suggests death to the unfortunate individual, who no longer hopes to escape what he considers to be his ineluctable fate."[86]

Some time later, Lévi-Strauss continues, the tribe solemnly celebrates the sacred rituals intended to send the accursed individual on his way into the realm of the dead. After the psychological terror of protracted isolation, exclusion from the community's fieldwork, hunting, and every other sort of participation in communal life, the "excommunicated" man once again stands in the centre of the collectivity, something which leads to a complete emotional overload: "Physical integrity cannot withstand the dissolution of the social personality".[87]

The anthropologist Cannon suggests that, in medical terms, the cause of death in these cases of ritual curses might be cardiac arrest induced by fear and shock.[88] The medical anthropologist Stumpfe, on the other hand, rather noted, in the cases of "psychogenic death" examined by him, a "slow, undramatic, peaceful passing away".[89] But regardless of the specific medical findings in the various cases and cultures, the fact remains that the phenomenon of "psychogenic death" that Kafka describes in his stories is no fiction but rather very much a part of our interpersonal reality.

But it is not just in remote or primitive societies that we see such forms of "social death". We also observe phenomena which correspond to Kafka's descriptions of "interpersonal death sentences" in Kafka's own 20th century in Europe. In the Nazi concentration camps the inmates were constantly given to understand, by their SS captors, that they were inferior beings not worthy of life. They too were declared "socially dead" even before they were killed. And indeed, this being the case, many camp inmates did lose their will to live. They became depressive, apathetic and sooner or later simply surrendered themselves to the fate decreed for them by the SS. If an inmate who had fallen into this state no longer appeared for the morning roll-call, he was immediately executed. For this reason, other inmates sometimes tried to force their "socially dead" co-inmates to pull themselves together, dragging them out bodily into the yard to answer the roll-call, but mostly in vain. We owe accounts of these terrible events to the psychoanalyst Bruno Bettelheim, who was himself an inmate in one of these camps.

Bettelheim reports that Communists and Social Democrats, as "political prisoners", were often better able to deal with the constant threat of death, since they knew themselves to be involved in a real active struggle against the Nazis and that, were they only given the chance, they would apply armed force against these latter. For the Jews, by contrast, it tended to remain completely incomprehensible why death should have been decreed to them in this way simply because they were Jews. They "internalized", so to speak, the message about themselves conveyed by the SS. These inmates "deteriorated into near autistic behaviour when the feeling of doom penetrated so deep that it brought the added conviction of imminent death. Such men were called 'Muslims' in the camps and other prisoners avoided them as if in fear of contagion. The connotation was that they had resigned themselves to death unresisting, as if this was the will of the SS (or of Allah)."[90]

In order to avoid this same thing happening to them, certain inmates resolved to form their own groups within the camp, encouraging and reinforcing one another mutually and creating, within the barracks to which they were confined, a "relational reality" of their own which allowed them to survive that unreality of being declared "dead before death" created by the SS.

But it was striking also, Bettelheim goes on, that,

even among the Jewish inmates, some were more able to deal with this declaration of "social death", others less able to deal with it. In the studies which he wrote after his liberation from the camps Bettelheim came to the conclusion that different people clearly possess different degrees of "certainty in being". Some people proved unable to maintain, under the constant threat of death, a sense of self-worth for very long at all; they broke down internally and suffered, even before they died, the "social death" decreed for them. Others, however, proved significantly more resistant. But why? Did some just naturally possess, perhaps for genetic reasons, a more stable "constitution of the self"? What forms, in the end, the core of our "sense of self"? What, indeed, is a "self"?

It was only years later that Bettelheim discovered, in connection with his researches on the phenomenon of autism, some answers to these questions. He noted some significant resemblances between the autistic children he was studying and the "Muslims" he had encountered in the concentration camps. In his 1967 book *The Empty Fortress*, still highly esteemed among psychologists,[91] he comes to the conclusion that autistic children must have undergone, very early in their lives, an experience much like that of the camp inmates: that of being "not wanted", not called upon to live, or even of being "wished dead". In order to survive this and to protect themselves against an overwhelming fear of death, they had built a wall around themselves and erected a sort of inner fortress. But since, Bettelheim goes on, the core of our "sense of self" develops, in this early phase of life, only through our interaction with our parents and through the recognition they accord us, the protective wall that these children are forced to erect around themselves is erected before they have had any chance to build up anything like this personal "core". The result is what Bettelheim calls an "empty fortress". This "empty fortress" ensures, indeed, the psychological survival of the children; but it leaves them lacking, in later life, any developed sense of self on which they can fall back, when needed. Such a developed sense of self is needed, however, if a human being is to maintain a living and trusting interaction with his or her fellow humans. Generally speaking, Bettelheim concludes, every human being, even perfectly mentally healthy ones, owes his or her later sense of self to this early mother-child relationship – which would, in turn, explain why some people possess a stronger vitality than others.

Although Bettelheim was able to achieve astonishing

results treating autistic children in his clinic, discussion still continues about the extent to which autism might, after all, be explicable in terms of genetic factors. What Bettelheim certainly has shown us, however, is that each human being is "tied together by ropes" with other human beings and needs the affirmation of his own existence provided to him by those with whom he is so bound. If the "ropes are cut" and this affirmation is suddenly withdrawn or if, in other words, one finds oneself declared "socially dead" by those around one, this will inevitably have fatal consequences:

> They (human beings) are tied together by ropes and it's bad enough when the ropes around an individual loosen and he drops somewhat lower than the others into empty space; ghastly when the ropes break and he falls.[92]

The existential dimension of a radical mutual dependence on one another comprises, of course, not only the possibility of the failure of human inter-relation, up to the point of the free fall of a living in "social death", but also the opposite possibility to this: that of entirely positive and enriching human inter-relations, something which Kafka never actually describes but which must be taken to be a notion latently foundational to all his stories. That drama of human failure which is described by him in all its facets can surely only take form against the background of a potential inter-human success. That is to say: human beings can always, potentially, acknowledge one another, trust one another and confirm and validate one another in each other's existence.

In his stories *The Metamorphosis* and *The Judgment* Kafka pointed up, with the phenomenon of "excommunication" in the family and the declaration of "social death" be it by father or by sister, the most extreme dimension of the inter-human, emphasizing its characteristics still further through the fictional form. Also in *A Hunger Artist* and *The Trial* the protagonist's systematic exclusion from society inevitably culminates in his death. In the latter work K. learns that his guilt can be recognized already by the shape of his lips, so that his ultimate condemnation is fixed from the very start. It might be objected, however, that these are only invented stories and correspond to no reality.

As a rule, none of us, at least today, are likely to find ourselves arrested one morning in our apartment, accused without proof, and executed. Nor are any of us likely to be "hunger artists", forgotten in a cage and starved to death. Nor, finally, are we likely to have the experience of being transformed overnight into a beetle, driven out of our family, and declared "socially dead". But what Kafka allows us to experience through these stories is a certain existential imperilment which can, at any moment, become social reality. Although anthropology and psychology have long since enlightened us as to the likely fatal consequences of such "excommunications" and declarations of "social death", this has not prevented such measures from being sometimes, as in staff and personnel matters for example, knowingly and wilfully applied.

A "human resources" department within a corporation may sometimes rid the latter of a no-longer-desired employee by organizing a sort of collective bullying or persecution. The company thus saves itself the severance pay by making the working environment so unpleasant for the employee that he resigns before he is dismissed. He is separated from his colleagues and assigned a meaningless job that does not challenge him until, for example, he takes to spending his work-hours surfing the Internet. If he is caught doing this, he is dismissed without severance pay, assuming he has not already suffered a breakdown through the psychological stress of the "excommunication".

Thus, one especially striking example of the decreeing of "social death" in modern society is what has been revealed, by investigations carried out by the French Public Prosecutors Office, to have occurred during the privatization of the French telecommunications company France Telecom. Such methods of deliberate persecution and alienation were indeed used in this case in order to accelerate staff cuts. Almost forty employees were proven to have been subjected to these measures, eighteen of whom, researchers discovered, committed suicide in the period between April 2008 and 2010 and another thirteen of whom made at least a suicide attempt. In total, some thirty-five employees killed themselves in the three-year course of the restructuring of the corporation. Didier Lombard, the head of the corporation at the time, is recorded as having stated at a meeting with employees: "I'm going to push this staff reduction through one way or another. These people can either leave through the door or out the window."[93] The company managers responsible for these campaigns of persecution were brought to trial and, although the legal situation at the time was still unclear, fines and even prison sentences were imposed.

But this is just one example of deliberately imposed "social death" sentences resulting in actual physical death. Even today, indeed, more than a decade after the France Telecom affair, only a minority of such cases have gone to trial but many other cases apt to do so could be mentioned. Taken together, they show that Kafka, in pointing up how every human being is existentially reliant on recognition and acknowledgment by the other human beings around him, really did put his finger on a fundamental truth about what it is to be a member of the human race. Man really does possess the power to "withdraw Man's right to existence", that is to say, to declare another member of the species effectively "dead" even before death actually overcomes them. But this in turn implies that Man also possesses the power to confirm and strengthen Man in existence and to preserve and promote, rather than destroy, members of the human species' lives. It is now time to look at this aspect of Kafka's philosophical discovery.

The Emperor's Language-Experiment, Modern Research into "Hospitalism", and Kafka's Truth

We find an especially striking piece of research into the significance of inter-personal relationships being carried out as early as the European Middle Ages by the great Hohenstaufen emperor, Frederick the Second, known to posterity as "the Amazement of the World". The contemporary chronicler, Salimbene da Parma, leaves us an account of events at Frederick's Sicilian court in the year 1285 which reveal this legendary Holy Roman Emperor's dual nature both as a pioneer of rational enquiry and enlightenment and as a kind of Nietzschean fusion of god and monster. Wishing to know which of the world's languages was the "natural language" spoken by human beings if they were not prompted to express themselves in any language by anybody else, he had new-born babies removed from their parents all over the different regions of his empire and gathered them together in a kind of children's home or hospital which was, admittedly, for the standards of the day a healthy and even luxurious place. The staff of the home, however, were instructed never to address a single word to the children. In Salimbene's own words:

"the foster-mothers and nurses were instructed to suckle and bathe and wash the children, but in no wise to prattle or speak with them; for he (the Emperor) would have learnt whether they would speak the Hebrew language (which had been the first), or Greek, or Latin, or Arabic, or perchance the tongue of their parents of whom they had been born. But he laboured in vain, for the children could not live without clappings of the hands, and gestures, and gladness of countenance, and blandishments."[94] A series of experiments by other potentates, which even employed, so as to be absolutely certain, foster-mothers and nurses who were deaf and dumb, all yielded the same fatal result.[95]

The psychoanalyst René Spitz also arrived, through his own pioneering researches into what he called "hospitalism"[96], at the conclusion that newborns and small children need far more in order to ensure their physical survival than just the satisfaction of their physical needs. He investigated the cases of children who had had, due to immune-system problems, to be kept in complete isolation for relatively prolonged periods. Separation from the mother in the early months of life, Spitz found, often led, even despite the excellent medical care the children were receiving, to fatalities, or at least to life-threatening traumas which, even if the children survived this phase, greatly impaired their flourishing in later life. After their stays in hospital the children were barely responsive to human speech, were disinclined to engage in play, began only very late to speak themselves and swung back and forth between apathy and aggression. In short, they suffered up to puberty and even beyond from serious psychological disturbances which, since Spitz's researches, have been known under the name of "hospitalism".

Both the cruel experiment of the Hohenstaufen emperor and the phenomenon of "hospitalism" clearly bear out the old wisdom to the effect that "Man does not live by bread alone". This saying, of course, is from the Bible and means, in the religious context, that human beings require, in order to survive and live in the fullest sense, not just material nourishment but the constant sustaining support of God. In the light of the emperor's experiment, however, and Kafka's discovery of the structure of interpersonal relations as a structure of radical mutual existential dependency, we may say that this saying acquires a second, humanity-focussed significance quite aside from all religion: Man does not live by bread alone; he must first be "called into existence" by other men and women.

Even a new-born baby, indeed, possesses already at birth all the systems required to sustain physical life. It can breathe, drink and call attention to itself when need be. Likewise inherent in every tiny human being is the potential to unfold and to develop. Thus, for example, every new-born has, from the moment of birth on, the universal capacity to learn any language under the sun. A baby born of Bavarian parents will, if he is brought up in a Chinese foster-family, learn to speak perfect Chinese, and vice versa. But first of all, these little human beings must be "called into life" in the way we have discussed.

The potential inherent in every new-born is in radical existential need of this "call into life". Kafka too recognized this. He writes in his diary:

It is entirely conceivable that life's splendour forever lies in wait around each one of us, in all its fullness […] If you summon it by the right word, by its right name, it will come.[97]

A human being, then, Kafka says, requires, if his life is to fully unfold and develop, that "the right word be spoken". This life, he himself, must be "called into existence":

This is the essence of magic, which does not create but summons.[98]

Kafka describes the existential "call into life" as a kind of "magic" because this call transforms latent predispositions into actual abilities. Moreover, this "magic" decidedly does not apply just to new-born babies but also to children, pubescents, or young adults. These groups of people often also need encouragement, a kind word, a mentor, in order to develop and exploit their own potential. Just this encouragement, Kafka tells us, was something he had sorely felt the lack of in his childhood and young years. His talent as a writer, which he recognized in himself very early on, was, as we have indicated, far from being encouraged, rather refused all confirming recognition by his father. It was this that led Kafka to the conclusion:

Every human being is peculiar and, by virtue of his peculiarity, called to play his part in the world. But he must have a taste for his own peculiarity. So far as my experience went, both at home and in school, the aim was to erase all trace of peculiarity.[99]

Kafka had, so he tells us in his diaries, never been able to develop any trust in himself or in his own abilities: the trust that would have been necessary for a healthy and normal life. Kafka's biographers are unanimous in holding that this early undermining of Kafka's confidence in himself went to aggravate an already morbid over-sensitivity and contributed to making Kafka, later in life, wary of other human beings almost to the point of reclusiveness. As a mature man, Kafka repeatedly emphasized how important it was to him to be alone. His entire literary work, he suggested, was something he owed to his withdrawal from the world:

> What I accomplished was only the result of being alone.[100]

One might suppose, from this remark, that Kafka made a conscious decision to lead a reclusive life, precisely in order to gain time for his writing. One often hears it said, in fact, that Kafka needed solitude in order to live out his creativity and really "get everything off his chest". But this is only half of the truth:

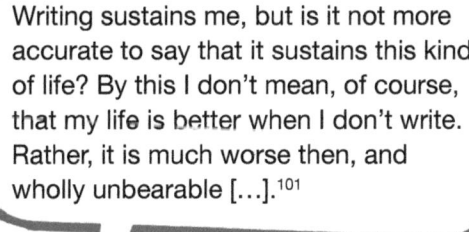

> Writing sustains me, but is it not more accurate to say that it sustains this kind of life? By this I don't mean, of course, that my life is better when I don't write. Rather, it is much worse then, and wholly unbearable […].[101]

Writing, says Kafka, sustains him in life and makes his life bearable. But these nightly sessions at the writing table, Kafka goes on in the same letter to say, are

[...] the reward for serving the devil [...] This descent to the dark powers, this unshackling of spirits bound by nature, these dubious embraces and whatever else may take place in the nether parts which the higher parts

no longer know, when one writes one's stories in the sunshine. Perhaps there are other kinds of writing, but I know only this one, at night [...].[102]

But another, more prosaic reason why Kafka wrote at night was because during the day he had to work. For fourteen whole years he worked, in the daytime, as a legal investigator of compensation claims at the Prague Workers' Accident Insurance Institute, even though his "sole desire", as he put it, was to be allowed to devote himself to his "scribbling", which had to be pursued at night. This life both laborious and lonely was not, however, one that he had really chosen for himself. He really had no option but to engage with these "dark powers". It should never be thought, however, that Kafka was happy in this state of extreme solitude. We find him writing, for example, to Max Brod:

> It is a long time since I have been plunged in inexplicable unhappiness [...] I am so urgently driven to find someone who will merely touch me in a friendly manner that yesterday I went to the hotel with a prostitute.[103]

Kafka's relations with women, in fact, never yielded, despite three engagements and much intense correspondence, any result in the form of marriage or even of any partnership lasting over a long period. Kafka finally decided to dissolve all these engagements, apparently opting in the end for a consistent solitude, even though he was constantly torn back and forth between this option and its contrary. His inner conflicts here come to expression, for example, in the draft for a story, later worked into one of the pieces of his 1912 collection *Meditation*, which we find scribbled into his diary for the year 1910. Here, he praises, on the one hand, employment, love, family and regular income as things that help one "hold one's own" against the world and that preserve one against destructive feelings while on the other conceding that they do so only "tentatively":

For without a centre, without a profession, a love, a family, an income, i.e. without holding one's own against the world in the big things – only tentatively, of course – [...] one cannot protect oneself from losses that momentarily destroy one.[104]

More famous even than many of Kafka's fictional works has become his long correspondence of over a thousand pages with Felice Bauer. In these more than five hundred letters one can see how genuinely and strenuously Kafka tried to build up a workable relationship with a beloved woman. But one also observes here how fundamentally incapable he was of doing so, and how a part of him did not even want to. To this extent, Kafka's path of solitude and withdrawal was less a conscious decision than the result of the sole thing that he was really, constitutionally, in a position to do:

I am, not only because of my external circumstances but even much more because of my essential nature a reserved, silent, unsociable, dissatisfied person [...] I lack all aptitude for family life except, at best, as an observer [...] A marriage could not change me, just as my job cannot change me.[105]

The entries in his diary, as well as the famous *Letter to the Father* and numerous other testimonies, all point up the fact that Kafka never developed, even as an adult, any sense of trust and confidence in himself sufficient to allow him to enter vigorously and resolutely into the normal life of the world. His unsuccessful struggle to achieve this, particularly as evidenced by the thousand pages of his *Letters to Felice*, has earned him the double-edged distinction of going down as "the great bachelor of world literature".[106]

But it was not only in his relations with women that Kafka displayed a painful diffidence. He also remained extremely diffident with regard to his own literary creations. He is reported to have once said to the best-known of his publishers, Kurt Wolff, the great promoter of the "Expressionist" literature of the German-speaking world with which Kafka was contemporary, that

I'll be more grateful to you for sending my manuscripts back to me than for publishing them.[107]

There may, it is true, be a slight element of affectation and false modesty in remarks like these. But we must remember that, if Kafka is right, then any confidence and belief in himself that a man may have in later life emerges and develops already in childhood within the framework of the child's inter-personal relations as he lives them. Because it is in this early phase that there is formed that which is later designated as the "self": that is to say, whatever it is that we fall back on whenever, in later life, it is a question of "self-confidence" or "self-awareness". The experiment of Frederick II described above, the "hospitalism" studies of René Spitz, and Bettelheim's investigations into autism have, in the end, a common core. They show us very clearly the reality-creating power of that "calling into being" which human beings perform for other human beings.

Where this "calling into being" is prevented from occurring at all, as in the emperor's experiment, the little human being simply dies. And where the "call" remains faint and minimal, interrupted or insufficient, as in the cases studied by Spitz or by Bettelheim, then a human being, although he survives, may have to struggle his whole life long in order to shore up what little "sense of self" he has developed.

Kafka's protagonists all seem to bear within themselves this fundamental fragility of being. They all lack what Bettelheim calls "ontological security", that is to say, a fundamental confidence in their own "right to be". Kafka understood this very well:

A man cannot live without a steady faith in something indestructible within him [...] One of the forms (of this) is the belief in a personal God.[108]

Another form of expression of such a steady faith is belief in one's own self, one's own infallibility and strength to will and act, qualities definitely possessed by Kafka's father. Kafka himself definitely did not possess this basic "trust in his own being" and was very far from feeling himself to be guided or protected by a higher power. Already at the age of twenty-one we find him complaining in a letter to his friend Max Brod that he lacks the "stalwart technique for living" that other people seem to possess:

On another day when I opened my eyes after a short afternoon nap [...] I heard my mother calling down from the balcony in a natural tone: 'What

are you up to?' A woman answered from the garden: ‚I‘m having my teatime in the garden'. I was amazed at the stalwart technique for living some people have.[109]

Kafka's Imperative: Recognize the Individuality and Potential of Every Human Being!

Kafka shows us, in his literary work and also by the example of his own biography, all that can go wrong in human inter-personal relations. But he thereby at least gives us implicitly to understand something of the forms that human relationships that "go right" would have to take. He recognizes, for example, very clearly the importance of early childhood for the con-stitution of a "sense of self":

Every human being is peculiar and, by virtue of his peculiarity, called to play his part in the world. But he must have a taste for his own peculiarity.[110]

Here, one thing is supremely important: to discover the "peculiarity", or unique individuality, of every child. Kafka demands this with especial vehemence because this particular form of "confirmation in being" had not been accorded to him, or had been accorded to him only in a very inadequate degree. One of his private notes reads:

My peculiarity was not accorded any recognition.[111]

He was forbidden, as a child, to read books in the evening. And when, around the age of fourteen, he made his first attempts at writing it was not only his father who showed incomprehension and rejection of these early literary efforts:

An uncle who liked to make fun of people finally took the page that I was holding only weakly, looked at it briefly, handed it back to me, without even laughing, and said to the others, who were following him with their eyes: 'The

usual stuff'. To me he said nothing [...] I remained seated as before over the now-useless page of mine but with one thrust I had in fact been banished from society.[112]

This lack of recognition was not without consequences:

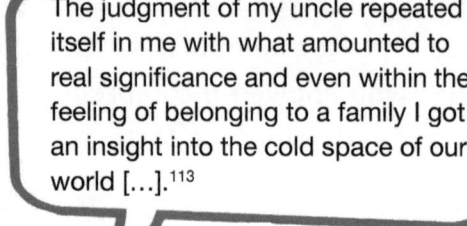

The judgment of my uncle repeated itself in me with what amounted to real significance and even within the feeling of belonging to a family I got an insight into the cold space of our world [...].113

If, over extended periods of time, a person receives no encouragement to develop their own individual talents and predispositions, this may not always result in a complete cessation of personal development but it can make this latter much harder:

[...] There is no doubt that I did not profit from my peculiarities with that true gain which finally manifests itself as permanent self-confidence [...].114

But of what use is this discovery of Kafka's for us to-day? Has it not become a cliché and a platitude by now that a child or a young person needs the support of parents and other "significant others" to develop and flourish? Have the effects of praise and blame, motivation and frustration, inhibition and encouragement not been known for many years to psychology, psychoanalysis and pedagogy? Have thinkers like Freud, René Spitz, and Bruno Bettelheim not, as we have seen, recognized the great significance of the "calling into being" that must occur in childhood?

Yes, it is true that the dynamics of human beings' "becoming what they are" are by now well-known. But Kafka showed us, already before Freud, Spitz or Bettelheim, yet one further dimension of this "becoming". He showed us, namely, that it is not only children who are exposed to situations like Spitz's "hospitalism" scenarios that tend to suffer difficulties later in life but also children from intact family situations, that is to say, definitely "wanted children". Kafka draws attention, in other words, to the often neglected fact that even "well-meaning" parents like his own do make, as a rule, errors in upbringing that have grave consequences:

> For parents do not stand in a free relationship to their children, as an adult stands toward a child – after all, they are his own blood, with this added grave complication: the blood of both the parents.[115]

Parents, Kafka believes, must look on "their own blood" as something quite special, as a part of themselves, their offspring, which they are now obliged to mould and form:

> When the father "educates" the child (it is the same for the mother) he will, for example, find things in the child that he already hates in himself and could not overcome, and which he now hopes to overcome, since the weak child seems to be more in his power than he himself. And so, in a blind fury, without waiting for the child's own development, he reaches into the depths of

the growing human being to pluck out the offending element. Or he realizes with horror that something which he regards as his own distinction is missing in the child [...] And so he begins to pound it into the child – which effort is successful, but at the same time disastrous, for in the process he pounds the child to pieces.[116]

Kafka addresses here the fundamental human problem at the heart of every education. The parents "mean well" when they aspire to see only their own best qualities, or those which they deem to be such, in their children and to pluck out those of their own weaknesses which they believe they perceive in their offspring. The child is expected to develop in a way entirely in accord with this loving care and attention. But precisely herein lies the danger: namely, that the child never gets to enjoy a "peculiar" development of its own. And just this, in the end, was the upshot of all Kafka's experiences.

Not just children who are unloved or insufficiently loved have difficulty in building up a coherent sense of self. Loved children too can become victims of attitudes of high expectation which – even if in a different way – still go to form obstacles to the child's own self-development. Kafka sums up, as he does so often, in a single sentence this dialectic of the "loving" education which, though well-meaning, ends up achieving the very opposite of its well-meant goal. The "loving" grown-up, says Kafka

[...] sees in the child only the loved thing, clings to the loved thing [...] His love prompts him to devour it.[117]

When Kafka complains that, due to the lack of recognition by his father, he was never able to develop his own uniqueness and "peculiarity" in any way that would bring him any real benefit, he points up for us just what is imperatively requisite for a truly flourishing human development. Quite aside from all the wishes we grown-ups may have with regard to his or her development, the tiny human being must be recognized and advanced in their own potentiality and individuality. What is needed, then, first of all here is an amazed perception and discovery of the child as a being in its own right with its own predispositions. This potentiality, which is at first almost invisible, giving only the faintest hints of its presence, can be activated or, as Kafka phrases it, "called into life":

It is entirely conceivable that life's splendour forever lies in wait around each one of us, in all its fullness, but veiled from view, deep down, invisible, far off. It is there, though, not hostile, not reluctant, not deaf. If you summon it by the right word, by its right name, it will come.[118]

In short, then: Kafka shows us, in his stories and novels, in the subtlest ways the failure and collapse of human inter-personal relations. His heroes turn into giant insects, suffer sentences of death from their own fathers, are driven from their place as helmsman, lie forgotten in cages, or find themselves accused and eventually executed by unknown authorities. Not a single one of these heroes succeeds in taking his destiny into his own hands. They are too lacking, in order to do this, in self-confidence and vitality. But behind each of these stories of failure lies a latent indication regarding the structure of a human inter-personal relation that would not fail or founder. In his autobiographical texts Kafka presents the message of his fictional works in still denser and more palpable form: no one can be their own sun; for better or worse, we are radically reliant upon one another; but we have at any moment the opportunity to see the "other" in his essential potentiality and to encourage this potentiality's development.

The philosopher Buber once formulated this key idea of Kafka's as follows: "The foundation of human being-with-others is this twofold and onefold: the desire of every human being to be confirmed in what he is, yes in what he is capable of becoming, by other human beings, and the capacity innate in Man for every individual to indeed do this service for his fellows."[119]

The literary author Kafka succeeded in transforming this abstract philosophical insight into sets of concrete images and situations which are much easier for all of us to grasp and appreciate. The "Kafkaesque" quality that we encounter in his stories is in fact something known to us from our dreams and sometimes, indeed, even from our real lives. It consists, essentially, in nothing else but the deep sense of discomfort and disorientation which arises from our failing to be perceived and confirmed as that which we are, and have the potential to be.

Kafka's Solace

Kafka is surely by far the most interpreted writer in the history of literature. In the century since his active years as a writer his work has generated over five million doctoral theses, scholarly essays and monographs. Enormously many words have been written about him; perhaps too many. But that Kafka's work seems still not to leave us in peace is surely a fact of great significance. Although he died very young, barely past forty, from tuberculosis, most likely himself destroyed a large part of what he had written, and left his only longer works, his three novels, in unfinished and fragmentary states,[120] he continues to fascinate us still today like almost no other writer. The reason for this is simple. Strange and surreal as they are, his stories and fragmentary novels contain a timeless truth that we cannot avoid confronting sooner or later. Kafka's message is one spoken very faintly – but one that cannot be ignored.

More brilliantly than any other writer, he showed up the dimension of terrible solitude that always exists against the background of that reality of existential relationality that is reality for every human being:

They (human beings) are tied together by ropes [...].[121]

If these ropes loosen, existence becomes difficult; if they break entirely, catastrophe ensues. Some people, indeed, feel more keenly than others what it is to be exposed to a "calling into being" by others that can be accorded or, alternatively, catastrophically refused. But all of us, to one extent or another, are familiar with that existential threat that arises from the possibility of an excommunication by our fellow men. Kafka points up with relentless clarity the sense of lack and loss that can blight our lives, the source of our feeling of alienation and spiritual homelessness – in a world to which we also long to belong and belonging to which, indeed, is absolutely indispensable to us.

Kafka's language has nothing sentimental about it. But it constantly evokes that most vital of sentiments and feelings: love. His stories allow us concretely to experience something which it would be impossible for any philosopher, writing as such, to make clear: the dimension of the lack of human comfort. He shows us the structure and essence of human inter-personal relation as one of the reciprocal assignation of being, although Kafka's showing of this structure is, in almost every case, the showing of its "deficient" forms: that is to say, of situations in which there is felt the painful lack of it.

Every one of his protagonists, without exception, is on a restless quest: a quest which, despite relentless effort, never achieves its goal. They are never able to really "arrive in life". Kafka offers no more to his readers than he does to his protagonists any "resolu-tion", any "turn for the better", any "happy ending". On the contrary, his stories draw us inexorably into a maelstrom of emotional homelessness. For all that, though, they convey to each of us a message that is not without solace, even if it is a faint solace.

It is this: Whoever finds, at the end of the day, that he has once again failed really to "arrive in life", or whoever awakens, in the morning, from a "Kafkaesque" dream, knows, thanks to Kafka, that he is not alone.

Bibliographical References:

1   The Diaries of Franz Kafka 1910-1913, edited by Max Brod, Secker
     and Warburg, 1948, p. 299.
2   Franz Kafka, Letters to Friends, Family and Editors, Schocken Books,
     New York, 1977, letter to Oskar Pollak of 20th of December, 1903.
3   Ibid. letter to Max Brod of 5th of July 1922.
4   Ibid.
5   The Diaries of Franz Kafka 1914-1923, edited by Max Brod, Secker
     and Warburg, 1948, p. 198.
6   Franz Kafka, Letters to Friends, Family and Editors, Schocken Books,
     New York, 1977, letter to Oskar Pollak of 9th of November, 1903.
7   Cited in Klaus Wagenbach, Kafka, Rowohlt Publishers, Reinbek, 1964,
     p. 33.
8   Oxford Advanced Learner's Dictionary, 2020.
9   Franz Kafka, Letters to Friends, Family and Editors, Schocken Books,
     New York, 1977, letter to Oskar Pollak of 27th of January, 1904.
10   Franz Kafka, The Metamorphosis and Other Stories, Oxford World's
     Classics, 2009, p. 29
11   Ibid. p. 36.
12   Ibid. p. 37.
13   Ibid.
14   Ibid. p. 42.
15   Ibid. p. 43.
16   Ibid. p. 51.
17   Ibid. p. 56.
18   Ibid.
19   Ibid. p. 59.
20   Ibid. p. 67.
21   Ibid. p. 68.
22   Ibid.
23   Ibid.
24   Ibid. p. 71.
25   Ibid.

26 Ibid. p. 74.
27 Ibid. p. 68.
28 Franz Kafka, Collected Stories, Schocken Books, New York, 1993, p. 411-12.
29 Ibid.
30 Ibid.
31 Ibid. p. 187-88.
32 Ibid. p. 189-90.
33 Ibid. p. 190.
34 Ibid. p. 192.
35 Ibid. p. 191.
36 Ibid. p. 193.
37 Ibid. p. 194.
38 Ibid. p. 198.
39 Ibid. p. 199.
40 Ibid.
41 Ibid. p. 200.
42 Ibid. p. 199.
43 Franz Kafka, The Trial, Oxford World's Classics, 2009, p. 5.
44 Ibid. p. 7.
45 Ibid. p. 8.
46 Ibid. p. 12.
47 Ibid.
48 Ibid. p. 33.
49 Ibid. p. 37.
50 Ibid. p. 38.
51 Ibid. p. 39.
52 Ibid. p. 77.
53 Ibid. p. 138.
54 Ibid. p. 152.
55 Ibid.
56 Ibid. p. 161.
57 Ibid. p. 165.
58 Ibid. p. 166.
59 Brod recounted this incident many years later, as a very old man, in a German radio interview given in the year of his own death, 1968.
60 Ibid. p. 125.
61 Ibid. p. 138.

62 Ibid. p. 8.

63 Ibid. p. 165.

64 Franz Kafka, Collected Stories, Everyman Library (edited by Gabriel Josipovici), 1993, p. 33.

65 Ibid. p. 35.

66 Ibid. p. 36.

67 Ibid. p. 38.

68 Ibid.

69 The Diaries of Franz Kafka 1910-1913, edited by Max Brod, Secker and Warburg, 1948, p. 278.

70 Ibid. p. 38.

71 Franz Kafka, Dearest Father: Stories and Other Writings, Schocken Books, New York, 1954, p. 142.

72 Ibid. p. 161.

73 Ibid.

74 Ibid.

75 Ibid. p. 203.

76 The present author has published, in German, an entire book-length study on this topic of the ontological structures of inter-personal relationships. See Walther Ziegler, Anerkennung und Nicht-Anerkennung. Studien zur Struktur zwischenmeschlicher Beziehung aus symbolisch interaktionistischer, existenzphilosophischer und dialogischer Sicht, Bouvier Publishers, Berlin 1992, especially pp. 160-75.

77 Franz Kafka, Letters to Friends, Family and Editors, Schocken Books, New York, 1977, letter to Oskar Pollak of 20th of December, 1903.

78 Franz Kafka, The Aphorisms, Schocken Books, 2015, p. 110.

79 Franz Kafka, The Trial, Oxford World's Classics, 2009, p. 164.

80 The Zürau Aphorisms of Franz Kafka, Schocken Books, New York, 2005, p. 77

81 Kafka, Nachgelassene Schriften I, edited by Malcolm Pasley, Fischer Publishers, Frankfurt, 2002.

82 Franz Kafka, The Metamorphosis and Other Stories, Oxford World's Classics, 2009, p. 22.

83 Ibid. p. 68.

84 Franz Kafka, Collected Stories, Everyman Library (edited by Gabriel Josipovici), 1993, p. 38.

85   See, for example, Klaus-Dietrich Stumpfe, Der Psychogene Tod; Stuttgart, 1973.

86   Claude Lévi-Strauss, Structural Anthropology, Basic Books, New York, 1963, p. 167.

87   Ibid. p. 168.

88   Walter B. Cannon, Voodoo Death, in American Anthropologist, Vol. 44, pp. 169-181, New York, 1942, p. 180.

89   See, Klaus-Dietrich Stumpfe in Curare, Vol. 8, Berlin, 1985, p. 232.

90   Bruno Bettelheim, The Empty Fortress, The Free Press, New York, 1967, p. 65.

91   Ibid. passim.

92   Franz Kafka, Letters to Friends, Family and Editors, Schocken Books, New York, 1977, letter to Oskar Pollak of 20th of December, 1903.

93   Newspaper reports also cited the company's Human Resources chief as saying that managers ought to "use psychological mechanisms" to "inspire in the workers the desire to start a new life somewhere else". He spoke of "targeted frustration". Many employees were, without being fired, given entirely new jobs. If they refused them, they were assigned to call-centre work or work in shops selling cellphones. Managers were evaluated on how massively they had managed to cut the workforce. Many resigning employees spoke explicitly of persecution in their resignation letters. "Corporate bullying" was not, indeed, a criminal offence in France at the time. Nevertheless, the case here was so grave that the company was eventually fined, and even prison sentences imposed, for these campaigns of persecution.

94   Salimbene's chronicle is cited on p. 382 of Bettelheim's The Empty Fortress.

95   Other such experiments are recorded in Egypt in the 6th century BC, and, after Frederick, in both the 15th and 16th centuries.

96   See René Spitz, "Hospitalism—An Inquiry Into the Genesis of Psychiatric Conditions in Early Childhood".

97   The Diaries of Franz Kafka 1914-1923, edited by Max Brod, Secker and Warburg, 1948, p. 195.

98   Ibid.

99   Franz Kafka, Dearest Father: Stories and Other Writings, Schocken Books, New York, 1954, p. 203.

100 The Diaries of Franz Kafka 1910-1913, edited by Max Brod, Secker and Warburg, 1948, p. 292.
101 Franz Kafka, Letters to Friends, Family and Editors, Schocken Books, New York, 1977, letter to Max Brod of July 5th, 1922.
102 Ibid.
103 Franz Kafka, Letters to Friends, Family and Editors, John Calder, London, 1978, p. 45 (letter of September 1908 to Brod).
104 The Diaries of Franz Kafka 1910-1913, edited by Max Brod, Secker and Warburg, 1948, p. 24.
105 Ibid. pp. 299-300.
106 The coinage is Reiner Stach's, in his German Kafka biography.
107 The remark is reported by Alois Prinz in another German biography of Kafka.
108 Franz Kafka, The Aphorisms, Schocken Books, 2015, p. 135.
109 Franz Kafka, Letters to Friends, Family and Editors, John Calder, London, 1978, p. 17 (letter to Max Brod of 28th of August 1904).
110 Franz Kafka, Dearest Father: Stories and Other Writings, Schocken Books, New York, 1954, p. 203.
111 Ibid.
112 The Diaries of Franz Kafka 1910-1913, edited by Max Brod, Secker and Warburg, 1948, p. 44.
113 Ibid.
114 Franz Kafka, Dearest Father: Stories and Other Writings, Schocken Books, New York, 1954, p. 204.
115 Franz Kafka, Letters to Friends, Family and Editors, John Calder, London, 1978, p. 295 (letter to Elli Hermann (née Kafka), autumn 1921).
116 Ibid.
117 Ibid. p. 280.
118 The Diaries of Franz Kafka 1914-1923, edited by Max Brod, Secker and Warburg, 1948, p. 195.
119 Martin Buber, I and Thou, Charles Scribner's Sons, New York, 1970, p. 88.

120 Perhaps the single most famous work of Kafka's, The Trial, remained very decidedly in a fragmentary state. Kafka really only produced, in his lifetime, clearly structured drafts of the book's beginning and end. He attempted to fill in the gaps with various episodes. But these pages were comprised within those "literary remains" which Kafka instructed the executor of his will, Max Brod, to destroy unpublished. Fortunately for us, Brod did not carry out this instruction, recognizing in the pieces too huge a literary worth and quality. Brod was the first to attempt to put the pieces together to form something like a complete novel but several other, alternative reconstructions have followed.

121 Franz Kafka, Letters to Friends, Family and Editors, Schocken Books, New York, 1977, letter to Oskar Pollak of 20th of December, 1903.

Already published in the same series:

Walther Ziegler
Adorno in 60 Minutes
ISBN 9783750460232

Walther Ziegler
Arendt in 60 Minutes
ISBN 9783752649031

Walther Ziegler
Buddha in 60 Minutes
ISBN 9-783-7543-5135-2

Walther Ziegler
Camus in 60 Minutes
ISBN 9783741227738

Walther Ziegler
Confucius in 60 Minutes
ISBN 9783753423128

Walther Ziegler
Descartes in 60 Minutes
ISBN 9-783-7562-1316-0

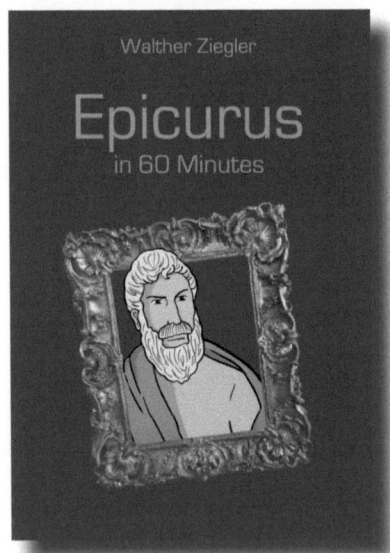

Walther Ziegler
Epicurus in 60 Minutes
ISBN 9-783-7562-9515-9

Walther Ziegler
Foucault in 60 Minutes
ISBN 978375342688

Walther Ziegler
Freud in 60 Minutes
ISBN 9783741227707

Walther Ziegler
Habermas in 60 Minutes
ISBN 9783752612370

Walther Ziegler
Hegel in 60 Minutes
ISBN 9783741227677

Walther Ziegler
Heidegger in 60 Minutes
ISBN 9783741227752

Walther Ziegler
Hobbes in 60 Minutes
ISBN 9783751968317

Walther Ziegler
Kafka in 60 Minutes
ISBN 9-783-7562-9519-7

Walther Ziegler
Kant in 60 Minutes
ISBN 9783741226373

Walther Ziegler
Marx in 60 Minutes
ISBN 9783741227691

Walther Ziegler
Nietzsche in 60 Minutes
ISBN 9783752803822

Walther Ziegler
Platon in 60 Minutes
ISBN 9783741227615

Walther Ziegler
Popper in 60 Minutes
ISBN 9783750470897

Walther Ziegler
Rawls in 60 Minutes
ISBN 9783750424050

Walther Ziegler
Rousseau in 60 Minutes
ISBN 9783741227622

Walther Ziegler
Sartre in 60 Minutes
ISBN 9783741227653

Walther Ziegler
Schopenhauer in 60 Minutes
ISBN 9783750498853

Walther Ziegler
Smith in 60 Minutes
ISBN 9783741227721

Walther Ziegler
Wittgenstein in 60 Minutes
ISBN 9783750426955

THE AUTHOR:

Dr Walther Ziegler is academically trained in the fields of philosophy, history and political science. As a foreign correspondent, reporter and newsroom coordinator for the German TV station ProSieben he has produced films on every continent. His news reports have won several prizes and awards. He has also authored numerous books in the field of philosophy. His many years of experience as a journalist mean that he is able to present the complex ideas of the great philosophers in a way that is both engaging and very clear. Since 2007 he has also been active as a teacher and trainer of young TV journalists in Munich, holding the post of Academic Director at the Media Academy, a University of Applied Sciences that offers film and TV courses at its base directly on the site of the major European film production company Bavaria Film. After the huge success of the book series "Great thinkers in 60 Minutes", he works as a freelance writer and philosopher.